ISRAEL IN THE PERIOD OF THE JUDGES

STUDIES IN BIBLICAL THEOLOGY

A series of monographs designed to provide the best work in biblical scholarship both in this country and abroad

Advisory Editors:

STUDIES IN BIBLICAL THEOLOGY

Second Series · 29

ISRAEL IN THE PERIOD OF THE JUDGES

A. D. H. MAYES

ALEC R. ALLENSON INC.

635 EAST OGDEN AVENUE

NAPERVILLE, ILL.

© *SCM Press Ltd 1974*

ISBN 0-8401-3079-1

Library of Congress Catalog Card No. 73-85127

Published by Alec R. Allenson Inc.
Naperville, Ill.
Printed in Great Britain

CONTENTS

PREFACE

The view that the Israelite tribes had an amphictyonic organization in the period of the judges has come under attack from several
directions in recent years. The following pages go back to a
doctoral thesis, submitted to the Faculty of Arts in the University
of Edinburgh in 1969, which was in part devoted to that subject.
The scale of my indebtedness to many writers will be evident to
those familiar with the relevant literature, even if I have inadver-
tently failed to acknowledge it in the notes. To a number of
scholars, however, I am particularly grateful. Professor J.
Weingreen and Dr E. W. Nicholson first aroused my interest in
the study of the Old Testament. In Edinburgh Professor N. W.
Porteous and Dr R. E. Clements were always generous with their
time and assistance. To Professor G. W. Anderson I am deeply
indebted, both for his guidance while I was in Edinburgh and for
his continued practical interest since then. Professor P. R. Ackroyd
kindly read the manuscript and made many helpful comments and
suggestions for improvement. Finally, I am grateful to my wife
Elizabeth for her help with the manuscript and the proofs.

Trinity College, Dublin
June 1973   A. D. H. Mayes

ABBREVIATIONS

AASOR	*Annual of the American Schools of Oriental Research*
ANET	*Ancient Near Eastern Texts relating to the Old Testament*, ed. J. B. Pritchard, 1950
ANVAO	Avhandlinger utgitt av Det Norske Videnskaps-Akademi i Oslo
ASTI	*Annual of the Swedish Theological Institute*
ATANT	Abhandlungen zur Theologie des Alten und Neuen Testaments
ATD	Das Alte Testament Deutsch
BA	*The Biblical Archaeologist*
BASOR	*Bulletin of the American Schools of Oriental Research*
BBB	Bonner Biblische Beiträge
BWANT	Beiträge zur Wissenschaft vom Alten und Neuen Testament
BZAW	Beihefte zur *Zeitschrift für die Alttestamentliche Wissenschaft*
CAH	*The Cambridge Ancient History*
CBQ	*Catholic Biblical Quarterly*
EvT	*Evangelische Theologie*
FRLANT	Forschungen zur Religion und Literatur des Alten und Neuen Testaments
HAT	Handbuch zum Alten Testament
HTR	*Harvard Theological Review*
HUCA	*Hebrew Union College Annual*
IB	*The Interpreter's Bible*
ICC	International Critical Commentary
IDB	*The Interpreter's Dictionary of the Bible*
IsrEJ	*Israel Exploration Journal*

JBL	*Journal of Biblical Literature*
JNES	*Journal of Near Eastern Studies*
JCS	*Journal of Cuneiform Studies*
JTS	*Journal of Theological Studies*
LXX	Septuagint (Greek translation of the Old Testament)
NedTTs	*Nederlands Theologisch Tijdschrift*
OTS	*Oudtestamentische Studiën*
OTWerkSuidA	*Die Ou Testamentiese Werkgemeenskap in Suid-Afrika*
PEQ	*Palestine Exploration Quarterly*
PJB	*Palästinajahrbuch*
RB	*Revue Biblique*
RGG	*Die Religion in Geschichte und Gegenwart*
SBT	Studies in Biblical Theology
SEÅ	*Svensk Exegetisk Årsbok*
ST	*Studia Theologica*
TGUOS	*Transactions of the Glasgow University Oriental Society*
TLZ	*Theologische Literaturzeitung*
VT	*Vetus Testamentum*
VTS	Supplements to *Vetus Testamentum*
WMANT	Wissenschaftliche Monographien zum Alten und Neuen Testament
ZAW	*Zeitschrift für die Alttestamentliche Wissenschaft*
ZDPV	*Zeitschrift des Deutschen Palästina-Vereins*
ZTK	*Zeitschrift für Theologie und Kirche*

INTRODUCTION

The subject for discussion here, and its importance for the reconstruction of the early history of Israel, is perhaps best introduced
and illustrated if reference is made to the ways in which the term
'Israel' is used by some of the prophets.[1] It is used extensively with
reference to the northern kingdom, and is in fact the name applied
to the northern tribes from the time that the monarchy established
by David disintegrated after the death of Solomon.[2] However, in
the prophetic books 'Israel' is also used with reference to Judah.[3]
It would perhaps be possible to explain this by arguing that after
the fall of the northern kingdom to the Assyrians in 721 BC, the
name Israel was transferred to Judah which was all that remained
of David's former empire. Such an argument, however, is too
simple since it fails to account satisfactorily for the necessity for a
transfer of name having taken place in the first instance. Moreover, this argument does not explain yet a third use of the name
Israel by the prophets. This is with reference not to the northern
nor to the southern tribes as separate units, but to both taken
together as the people of Yahweh. This use of the term is found in
the words attributed to prophets who lived after, and perhaps also
with those who lived before, the fall of the northern kingdom.[4]
That these prophets, when they use the term Israel in this way, are
in most cases referring to the past history of the people or to the
future, rather than to the present, does not alter the fact that they
knew of and could use the designation Israel of all the people of
Yahweh regardless of whether they lived in the northern or the
southern kingdom. This being the case, it is most probable that in
those passages where the name Israel is applied to Judah, here
Judah should be understood not as the southern kingdom over

against the northern kingdom but as the only surviving part of
that greater entity Israel – the whole people of Yahweh. Yahweh
is not known as the God of Judah, or the God of Ephraim; he is
the God of Israel, the Holy One of Israel. This Israel is not the
people of the northern tribes or of the southern tribes but of both
together united by their common allegiance to Yahweh. In the
view of the prophets, then, the people Israel has a unity which
supersedes its political divisions.

The problem here is to account for this idea, to find the origin
of this comprehensive use of the name Israel. First of all, two
points must be made. From what has already been said it is clear
that the question at issue concerns mainly the relation between the
northern kingdom and the southern kingdom. At least from the
death of Solomon onwards these were two separate and independent political entities, sometimes at peace but more often in a
state of war with each other. That they could be treated by the
prophets as the one people of Yahweh, albeit in a strictly religious
way, reflects a traditional religious unity which must reach back
before the time that the separate states were founded. The unity
of Israel as the people of Yahweh is a religious unity, and so our
aim must be to bring to light historical conditions which will
provide an explanation for the fact that this Yahwistic faith was
common to both north and south.[5] Secondly, it is to be noted that
the search for such historical conditions is not identical with an
investigation into the origin of the name Israel. Where this name
originated, and how it came to be applied to the people which had
Yahweh for its God, are still unsolved questions,[6] which, however, are not of primary importance for our purposes. Our concern is with the origin of the unity of the people of Yahweh, both
north and south; that this people bore the name Israel can thus be
taken in large measure as incidental to our main theme. Its significance here lies only in its application to the people which found
its unity in having Yahweh for its God.

In the search for the origin of this unity only a brief stop need
be made with the monarchy of David and Solomon since it is clear
that this period cannot provide the historical conditions in the
framework of which such unity could have been founded. The
state which David established was not a national but a territorial
one, and the dualism of the northern and southern kingdoms,
which becomes so apparent after the death of Solomon, really

goes back at least into the time of David.[7] The Davidic empire, which included not only the northern and southern tribes but also the territories which until the time of David had been inhabited by the former Canaanite population of Palestine as well as foreign countries such as Edom, Moab and Ammon, was united only in the person of David himself; and, while it may have been David's ultimate aim to weld these heterogeneous components of his empire into a national state, this cannot be seen as the starting point for the growth of the idea of Israel as the people of Yahweh.

At first sight the time of Saul seems to present conditions favourable to the origin and growth of Israel as the people of Yahweh. Saul became king over a group of tribes. His rule did not extend, as that of David did, to include those areas of Palestine still occupied by the Canaanites,[8] not to mention independent countries on the borders of Palestine. Some difficulty has been felt in determining the position of Judah in the time of Saul. Thus, it is sometimes argued that it is far from certain that Judah formed part of Saul's kingdom, but that II Sam. 2.9, where Gilead, Asher, Jezreel, Ephraim and Benjamin are specifically mentioned as the territory over which Saul's son Ishbosheth was made king, should be taken as giving the true extent also of the kingdom of Saul.[9] However, the evidence is very strongly against any such general assertion on the basis of this verse. There is abundant indication that at least during some part of Saul's reign Judah formed part of his kingdom.[10] In particular, there is the expedition which Saul undertook against the Amalekites living to the south of Judah. This necessarily involved passing through Judah where, in the area of Carmel to the south of Hebron, Saul afterwards erected a victory stele.[11] Probably the battle was undertaken in the first place for the relief of Judah. Furthermore, the fact that David, a Judean, feared for the safety of his parents in Judah after his break with Saul,[12] and the fact that he himself was eventually forced to flee to the Philistines,[13] and also the fact that he was considered by Saul a rival to the succession of Jonathan to the throne, all testify to Judah's having formed part of Saul's kingdom. But in spite of this, it is doubtful that the period of Saul's kingship should be considered as the time of origin of that Israel which transcended the boundaries of the tribes. This is for two reasons. In the first place, the length of Saul's reign was probably too short[14] for the unity of this Israel to have been founded and for it to have taken

such firm root that it could survive the changes in the structure of
the monarchy which became more and more apparent from the time
of David on, and not only reappear in the words of the classical
prophets, but also dominate the present form of many of the Pentateuchal traditions.[15] In the second place, rather than that the unity
of Israel should have been founded in the period of Saul, it appears
much more probable that Saul's rule over the Israelite tribes presupposes that unity which is manifest in the prophets' address to
Israel as the people of Yahweh.

These considerations force us back to the period before the
monarchy in the search for the origin of Israel's unity. It is with
this period that we shall be concerned in the following pages, and,
in particular, our main task will be to deal thoroughly with the
reconstruction which Noth[16] has made of this time. In Noth's
view, Israel before the advent of the monarchy was a federation of
twelve tribes constituted on the pattern of the later Greek amphictyonies. This theory has not only illuminated and given order to
a rather obscure part of Israel's history, but it has also provided the
ideal background and framework for our understanding of what
Israel really was. Israel was a sacral confederacy of twelve tribes
united in the worship of Yahweh at a common sanctuary; the
monarchy which came later was something extraneous to this tribal
organization; but the latter was not supplanted by the monarchy
completely; Israel, as the people of Yahweh, lived on after the
period of the judges in which it originated, and formed a link
bringing together those parts of the people which were separated
by political structures.

While this view has been rejected by some scholars, it has been
accepted in one form or another by most, and has come to form
the basis of much recent work dealing with the origin and development of Israelite religion and law which were normative for the
nation from that time on. Perhaps even for this reason alone, but
especially because the word 'amphictyony', which Noth took from
the Greek organizations and applied to the Israelite tribal structure, has become a catchword without much thought being taken
for what it implies, it is time that the whole theory be examined
afresh in the light of some more recent work, so that it may be
determined in what form, if at all, the organization which Noth
has proposed may fit the facts which are at our disposal for this
time.

The period with which we are concerned here is the period of the judges, which is covered by the early part of the deuteronomistic historical work.[17] This work extends from Deuteronomy to II Kings and was, following the date of the last event recorded in it, composed probably shortly after the release of king Jehoiachin from prison in exile in 561 BC, that is, some five hundred years after the period of the judges. For his representation of the early period the deuteronomistic historian had many sources available and, as far as the Books of Joshua and Judges are concerned, it is in most places fairly easy to distinguish the contribution of the deuteronomistic historian, written in a distinctive style, from the traditions which he used and edited for his work. One thing which is particularly evident here is that it is precisely in the deuteronomistic sections that we find all Israel involved in the events related, while in the actual traditions which the deuteronomist has used only a small part of this Israel takes part. This is especially clear in those narratives in the Book of Judges which deal with the wars waged by the charismatic deliverers. In each case these wars involved only one or two of the tribes, but to the traditions about them the deuteronomist has added a framework which sets the events related in an all-Israel context. Less obvious instances of the same thing may be found in the Book of Joshua where, for example, the conquest story of chs 2–9 is set in an all-Israel context while the actual traditions themselves centre on events taking place almost exclusively within the area settled by the tribe of Benjamin. So Josh. 2–9 may originally have been the particular conquest tradition of the tribe of Benjamin which has only at a secondary stage of its history been treated as the conquest story of all Israel.

There are two main possible effects of this work of the deuteronomist which must be kept in mind: (1) by giving an all-Israel context to originally local traditions the deuteronomist has not only given a wider reference to these traditions but he has forced on them what in many places may be a false chronology; that is, local traditions which may originally have told of events which took place simultaneously have been represented as relating events involving all Israel which took place successively; (2) this false chronology may affect not just one or two isolated events but the whole representation of the period of the judges; our understanding of the very existence of 'the period of the judges' may be based simply on a deuteronomistic reconstruction, so that it may in fact be more likely that, as far as the actual history is concerned, we should think in terms, not of a clearly defined conquest of the land followed by a distinct period of the judges which in turn gave way to the monarchy, but rather of a continuous process of settlement in the land which extended from the time of the first appearance of an Israelite tribe in the land up to the election of Saul as king.[18] This would involve treating the wars recounted in the Book of Judges not simply as the defensive wars of a well-settled Israel but as part of this process by which the tribes gradually established themselves in their settlements. However, before such conjectures as these can be entertained, the subject with which we are mainly concerned here – that of the possible amphictyonic organization of Israel in the period of the judges – must be investigated.

In what follows no attempt is made to give a full account of every view on the subject. Instead, the researches of many scholars have been used in order to give an over-all presentation which in its general outline if not in its detail will, I hope, fairly represent a considerable tendency within this particular area of Old Testament studies.

I

THE THEORY OF THE AMPHICTYONY

Israel, according to Noth, was a confederacy of twelve tribes which came into existence in Palestine in the time before the foundation of the monarchy. Before this time no twelve-tribe confederacy called Israel existed, and indeed not even the tribes as such existed before the settlement in Palestine. What we have to imagine are separate and independent clans and families wandering on the desert fringes. After settlement in Palestine these clans and families came together to form tribes, and the tribes came together to form a federation. This was a very gradual process.[1] The evidence for the existence of this federation which eventually emerged is drawn from a variety of sources, both within and outside the Old Testament, though the extra-biblical evidence is mainly used to supplement and confirm the picture which is derived from the Old Testament.

Israel, as a group of twelve tribes, was in no way peculiar, for the Old Testament itself mentions several other groups of either twelve or six tribes: Gen. 22.20–24 tells of twelve Aramean tribes descended from the twelve sons of Nahor, eight by his wife and four by his concubine; Gen. 25.13–16 gives the names of twelve sons of Ishmael who are clearly tribal eponyms; Gen. 36.10–14 names the twelve sons of Esau who are eponyms of Edomite tribes; Gen. 25.2 gives the names of six Arabic tribes descended from Abraham through Keturah; and Gen. 36.20–28 probably originally told of six Hurrian tribes.[2] Little, however, can be said on any of these except that the traditions of these tribal groupings probably derive from a time before the tribes in question had properly organized themselves into states.[3] But as far as the Israelite tribes are concerned, the Old Testament offers more detail.

The Old Testament pictures Israel as a community of twelve tribes descended from the twelve sons of Jacob. These sons are the eponyms of the Israelite tribes. In various passages in the Old Testament there are lists of these sons of Jacob/Israelite tribes. The lists are not identical but vary in some respects. One variation is of major importance: in some of the lists Levi is included while in others he is omitted. On the basis of this variation, then, the lists may be classified broadly into two main groups: on the one hand, there are those lists which number Levi among the tribes, and, on the other hand, there are those lists which omit Levi. Of the former group the two most important lists are to be found in the blessing of Jacob in Gen. 49 and in the story of the birth of the sons of Jacob in Gen. 29.31ff. In Gen. 49 the order of names is: Reuben, Simeon, Levi, Judah, Zebulun, Issachar, Dan, Gad, Asher, Naphtali, Joseph and Benjamin. In Gen. 29.31ff. the sons of Jacob are arranged as sons of Jacob's wives Leah and Rachel and of their handmaids Bilhah and Zilpah, in the following way: first are given four of Leah's sons: Reuben, Simeon, Levi, Judah; next, the two sons of Bilhah: Dan, Naphtali; then follow the two sons of Zilpah: Gad, Asher; then, two more sons of Leah: Issachar, Zebulun;[4] and, finally, Rachel's son: Joseph. There is no notice in the present form of the list of the birth of Benjamin. However, probably originally reference was made to Benjamin. but this notice was omitted by a redactor because of the presence, in Gen. 35.16–20, of an independent, local tradition on the birth of Benjamin.

All the other lists of the sons of Jacob which belong to this group which includes Levi, such as Deut. 27.12f. and others, show themselves, because of the order in which the names are given, to be dependent on the story of the birth of the sons of Jacob in Gen. 29.31ff.[5] Of the two lists in Gen. 49 and Gen. 29.31ff., the former must be understood to be the older from a literary point of view. They both agree in delineating two fixed groups within the twelve names: the sons of Leah and the sons of Rachel; however, in its separation of Issachar and Zebulun from the rest of the sons of Leah, and in its assignment of four tribes to the two handmaids, the account in Gen. 29.31ff. must be taken as a literary creation the details of which cannot be valued as old tradition from which historical conclusions may be drawn on the life of the Israelite tribes and their relation to one another.

The lists of tribes belonging to the second group do not include Levi. Apart from this, another difference between this type of list and the first group is that the lists of the second group deal with the tribes as such, while the lists of the first group deal with the tribal eponyms in most cases. The lists of the second group, of which the oldest and most important is to be found in the record of families in Israel in Num. 26.5–51, having omitted Levi, make up the number twelve of the tribes by dividing Joseph into Manasseh and Ephraim.[6] The list of tribes in Num. 26, where Gad has been transferred from near the end to take the place of Levi, appears in this order: Reuben, Simeon, Gad, Judah, Issachar, Zebulun, Manasseh, Ephraim, Benjamin, Dan, Asher, Naphtali. There are other tribal lists belonging to this second group in Num. 1, 2, 7, 10 and 13; but with the exception of the last mentioned all of these derive ultimately from Num. 1.5–15. This is an old list, and independent of Num. 26 since it presents the order Ephraim-Manasseh, rather than Manasseh-Ephraim. On the other hand, the late list in Num. 13, which has the order Manasseh-Ephraim, appears to be dependent on Num. 26. Of this group, therefore, the two basic lists are to be found in Num. 1.5–15 and Num. 26.5–51. Of these two the latter must be judged the older. The story of the blessing by Jacob of the two sons of Joseph in Gen. 48 reveals that it was the prominence of Ephraim in power and importance which brought about the change from the old order Manasseh-Ephraim to the new order Ephraim-Manasseh.

Aside from these two groups of lists there are others, such as I Chron. 12.25–38 (EVV vv. 24–37); 27.16–22 and also Deut. 33; but these can safely be left out of account. They show a breakdown of the twelve-tribe system, while the passages in I Chronicles seem also to be based on an attempt to combine the two tribal systems represented by the lists of the two groups already dealt with.[7] Thus, we are left with Gen. 49 and Num. 26 as the most important and original groupings of the tribes.

As for the time of origin of these lists, at least their relative dating can be quickly established. From the fact that Levi is included in Gen. 49 and omitted in Num. 26 it can be concluded fairly certainly that the system of tribes represented by the blessing of Jacob is older than that represented by Num. 26. For in the unlikely event of its being the other way round one would have to understand that Levi as a late-comer into the system of tribes deposed Gad from third place to a position fairly near the end.[8] On the other hand, if the system represented by Gen. 49 is the earlier it is possible to explain how Levi came to be omitted. Genesis 49.5–7, as well as the story of Gen. 34, reckon Levi as a 'secular' tribe alongside the other tribes. Apart from these passages Levi never appears in this capacity. Otherwise Levi is solely a priestly tribe to which no land is assigned in the territorial lists of areas inhabited by the tribes in Palestine. Thus, it can be concluded that the inclusion of Levi in Gen. 49 presupposes conditions of a very early time of which we have no accurate historical knowledge, while the ommission of Levi from the system, as in Num. 26, reflects the actual circumstances of the period about which we are better informed.[9] Therefore, Gen. 49 preserves the tradition of a tribal system which antedates the system presupposed by the list in Num. 26.

An absolute dating for the lists is made possible by a consideration of Num. 26. This list[10] refers to the tribe of Manasseh and so must come from a time later than the Song of Deborah in Judg. 5 where Manasseh is still not an independent tribe. On the other hand, it must be dated earlier than 733 BC when Israel was first incorporated within the Assyrian provincial system. The further observation that in the list none of the great and well-known Canaanite city-states of the plains are mentioned, while only a few of the Canaanite cities of the mountains are referred to, would point to a time of origin for the list when Israel did have possession of some of the mountain cities but had not yet ventured on to the plains of Palestine. Since this reflects the situation of the period of the judges, before the Canaanite city-states of the plains had been incorporated within Israel by David,[11] the list of Num. 26 may be assigned to some time in the second half of the period of the judges, after the Song of Deborah and before the time of David.

The list of Gen. 49, on the other hand, in its present form probably belongs to the time of David or Solomon.[12] But its present form is ultimately the responsibility of a collector who has gathered together originally independent sayings about the individual tribes. However, this is not to say that the present order of tribes in this list is a pure invention on the part of this collector. Instead, it goes back to a system of tribes which was familiar to him, a system which, Noth has argued, antedates the system presupposed in Num. 26. So, while Gen. 49 in its present form dates from the time of David or Solomon, it goes back ultimately to the early period of the judges. Thus, Noth has found in these lists evidence of a structure of the Israelite tribes which existed in the period of the judges, and which changed slightly in form during this period. It is this change in form which is reflected in the two different lists of Gen. 49 and Num. 26.

In these two tribal lists there are two fixed groups: the Leah tribes and the Rachel tribes. While these groups are designated in this way in the birth story in Gen. 29.31ff., they can also be recognized as groups in Gen. 49 by the order in which the names of the tribes appear. This grouping is then confirmed by the list of Num. 26 where Gad has been transferred to the place formerly occupied by Levi in order to retain the number six of the Leah group of tribes. The existence of a fixed group of Leah tribes within the organization of twelve tribes cannot be explained from conditions in the period of the judges, and so it must be assumed that the Leah tribes formed a fixed group in the land before the system of twelve tribes was established, that is, before the settlement of the 'house of Joseph' which, with Benjamin, formed the Rachel group of tribes.

Proceeding from this basis, Noth has attempted to describe the precise historical realities which are reflected in these tribal lists. It is at this point that use is made of information from classical sources on the amphictyonies of Italy and especially those of Greece.[13] There were a number of these amphictyonies, and each one usually had twelve members.[14] Of these it is the amphictyony centred round the two sanctuaries of Demeter at Pylae and Apollo at Delphi which is taken as the pattern. This is simply because it is about this amphictyony that most information has been preserved. Originally, this amphictyony only had one sanctuary, that of Demeter at Pylae, but later the sanctuary of Apollo at Delphi also came under its protection, and in time, because of the fame of Delphi as a place of oracle giving, the sanctuary of Apollo surpassed the original amphictyonic sanctuary in significance.[15] The organization of the amphictyony according to tribes confirms its very early origin; the city-states were only included in the amphictyony as representatives of particular tribes.

From the records handed down it can be seen that one of the chief tasks of the amphictyony was the care and maintenance of the central sanctuary. Here periodic festivals took place which were the occasion for a united gathering of the members of the amphictyony. However, the amphictyony was not founded for the purpose of looking after such a sanctuary. This is clear from the fact that in many cases it can be shown that a particular sanctuary had its own history before it became the central sanctuary of an amphictyony.[16] So the adoption of a central sanctuary presupposes an already existing alliance of the amphictyonic members. However, since local sanctuaries exercise a dividing rather than a uniting force, the adoption of a common sanctuary would have been a practical necessity for an amphictyony which had been founded for other reasons. The actual basis for the foundation of an amphictyony cannot be given with any certainty; our present state of knowledge will allow us to conclude only that it must have been mutual historical experiences, perhaps together with the need for resistance against a common enemy, which brought the tribes together.

The association which was thus established was a loose one, within which internecine warfare was not unknown.[17] However, the members of the amphictyony were under certain obligations: each member had to send a representative to the assemblies, and to contribute to the material upkeep, and to the defence in case of threatened violation, of the sanctuary. Few regulations governing the mutual relations of the amphictyonic members have been preserved,[18] but the infringement of such regulations would lead to the declaration of war against the offending member by the rest of the amphictyony.

This, then, is the organization, the Greek amphictyony, which Noth finds to be a valid parallel by which to elucidate the structure of the early Israelite tribal federation. It is only by presupposing the existence of such an amphictyony that the subsequent unity of the Israelite tribes under Saul can be explained, a unity which could not have been founded or preserved solely on the basis of the 'abstract concept' of Yahwism as the unifying factor.[19]

The Israelite amphictyony was founded at the entry of the 'house of Joseph' into the land. This was the group led by Joshua, and at the time of its entry the Leah tribes, the so-called concubine tribes, and the tribe of Benjamin, were already settled in the land. It was the incursion of the house of Joseph under Joshua which probably led directly to the foundation of the amphictyony of twelve tribes. This foundation was not such a startling innovation as might at first appear, for it seems that before this time there had already existed an amphictyony composed of the Leah group of six tribes.[20] Thus, the settlement of the house of Joseph brought about the extension of the old amphictyony of six tribes into one consisting of twelve members. The appearance of the house of Joseph provided the occasion for the inclusion also of other tribes outside the Leah group, within the amphictyony in order to make up the number of its members to twelve.

The record of the foundation of this amphictyony of twelve tribes is now to be found in Josh. 24.[21] According to the original form of the tradition now enshrined here, Joshua as leader of the house of Joseph, which had already previously acknowledged Yahweh as their God at the covenant ceremony at Sinai, now confronted those tribes which had settled in Palestine relatively early and had never been in Egypt. The 'parliament' of Shechem, reflected in Josh. 24, established the amphictyony and marked the end of the long process of the Israelite settlement in the land.

As well as this, however, Josh. 24 also preserves the memory of the foundation of an institutional, common form of cultic worship by which the tribes acknowledged the lordship of Yahweh. This form of worship was the celebration of the covenant between Yahweh and the amphictyonic Israel.[22] Since the tradition localizes this event at Shechem it must also be understood that it was this sanctuary which remained as the central sanctuary of the amphictyony. It was this sanctuary which the amphictyonic members had the obligation to maintain; so it was for purely practical reasons that the amphictyony numbered twelve members – each member had the charge of the sanctuary for one month in the year.[23]

At Shechem, therefore, where the ark found its first home,[24] the twelve tribes of Israel united in periodic covenant worship of 'Yahweh the God of Israel'.[25] Yahweh became the God of the amphictyony under the influence of the house of Joseph, an influence which may be accounted for not only by the strength of the house of Joseph but perhaps also by contact before settlement between it and the earlier amphictyony of the six Leah tribes.[26] But besides being a place of regular worship of Yahweh in the form of a covenant ceremony, it is also to be understood that the central sanctuary at Shechem was, as with the Greek amphictyonies, the meeting place of the tribal representatives[27] who came together to debate matters of general concern.

A further point of comparison with the Greek amphictyonies
is in the matter of law. Just as the Greek amphictyonies had their
amphictyonic law which regulated the common cult and probably
also the mutual dealings and relations of members, so too in
Israel. Parts of this amphictyonic law are now probably to be
found in the book of the covenant in Ex. 20.22–23.33,[28] and it is
likely that the book of the covenant as a whole took its origin
within the framework of the amphictyony. But besides this codified
law of the amphictyony, there also existed unwritten law,[29] and it
was for the violation of this unwritten law that there took place
the war of the tribes with the Benjaminite city of Gibeah, recounted
in Judg. 19–21. This event is paralleled in Greek history, in the
Amphissa war of 339 BC when the members of the amphictyony
called on the Locrians to punish the inhabitants of the city of
Amphissa, which lay in the province of the Locrians, for a cultic
offence. Instead, as with Benjamin and the inhabitants of Gibeah,
the Locrians declared themselves at one with the city of Amphissa,
thus bringing about an amphictyonic war which resulted in the
exclusion of the Locrians from the amphictyony.

In arguing thus for the existence of an amphictyony in Israel,
Noth disagrees with the view that the southern tribes of Judah
and Simeon had no connection with the northern tribes until the
time of the monarchy. However, Noth does agree that the southern
tribes stood in a peculiar position. There were six of them in all –
Judah, Caleb, Othniel, Cain, Jerahmeel and Simeon – dwelling on
the mountains of Judah, and the united appearance of these tribes
at the time of David's elevation to the kingship at Hebron points
to the possibility of there having existed an amphictyony of six
tribes in the south with Hebron as its central sanctuary. Thus,
Judah and Simeon would have belonged to two independent
amphictyonies, the one consisting of six tribes with its centre at
Hebron, and the other consisting of twelve tribes with its centre
at Shechem. In this, however, the organization of the Israelite
tribes would not be unique since the same thing is found in Greek
history where, for example, Athens belonged to three different
tribal federations.

II

THE ISRAELITE AMPHICTYONY

In our examination of the possibility of the existence of an amphictyony in ancient Israel, as proposed by Noth, all the evidence which has been adduced in favour of it must be considered. Since the evidence which is available is circumstantial, it does not seem possible to claim any one aspect of the theory of the amphictyony, such as the central sanctuary,[1] or the number twelve of the tribes,[2] as the basis of the theory on which its validity or invalidity rests. It is true that since the meaning of the word 'amphictyony' indicates an organization in which people were settled or dwelt around a focal point,[3] the primary characteristic of the Greek amphictyony was the central sanctuary. The name of the organization expressed a relationship, not primarily between the members of the organization themselves, but between the members and the sanctuary; therefore, the actual number of members was a secondary feature. This could lead to the conclusion that, in that Noth brought forward the tribal lists as his main evidence for an Israelite amphictyony, there is here a basic weakness in the theory which should have been based first of all on the records associated with Israel's sanctuaries. However, on the other hand, it might also be argued that the nature of the Old Testament evidence is determined by the nature of the records preserved in the Old Testament, and that, consequently, any weakness such as this in the analogy between Greece and Israel may be ascribed to the interests and emphasis of the Old Testament recorder rather than to actual differences between the Greek and Israelite organizations. Therefore, since all the various points which Noth made in his original publication, together with additional material brought forward by Noth and others later, have, in their cumulative effect, given rise to and apparently confirmed the view that Israel in the period of the judges was constituted in the form of an amphictyony, account must be taken here of all these separate points.[4] We begin, as did Noth, with the Old Testament evidence offered in the tribal lists.

A. *The Tribal Lists*

Apart from the late lists of tribes in I Chron. 12.25–38 (EVV vv. 24–37); 27.16–22, and the unique collection presented in the early Song of Deborah in Judg. 5, all the remaining lists, including Deut. 33, have the characteristic in common that they show a concern to preserve the number twelve of the tribes. In order to demonstrate, however, that the lists presuppose the historical existence in the period of the judges of systems of tribes corresponding to these lists, it is necessary first that the lists be shown to derive from or be based on prototypes or traditions which belong to this period, and secondly that such systems should correspond to historical data of this period which may be gleaned from other sources.

It may be agreed that the lists of tribes can be divided roughly into two groups, namely, those which include Levi and those in which Levi is omitted. For Noth it is the latter group which is of central importance in the question of the relative and the absolute dating of the lists, and so it should be discussed first. Lists in which Levi is absent are to be found in Num. 1.5–15, 20–43; 2.3–31; 7.12–83; 10.14–28; 13.4–15 and 26.5–51. However, even within this group significant differences are apparent, and it is these which can be used to determine which is the primary list and which are derivative. In Num. 2, 7 and 10 the order in which the tribes appear is identical: Judah, Issachar, Zebulun, Reuben, Simeon, Gad, Ephraim, Manasseh, Benjamin, Dan, Asher, Naphtali. In giving this order Num. 7 and 10 are clearly dependent on Num. 2 which, in describing the way in which the people encamped, provides the background of and the reason for this particular order of tribes.[5] The camp was laid out, following the four points of the compass, in four groups of three tribes: thus, to the east there was the camp of Judah comprising the tribes of Judah, Issachar and Zebulun; to the south was the camp of Reuben comprising the tribes of Reuben, Simeon and Gad; to the west was the camp of Ephraim comprising the tribes of Ephraim, Manasseh and Benjamin; and to the north was the camp of Dan comprising the tribes of Dan, Asher and Naphtali. On the other hand, Num. 1.20–43 presents the following order of tribes: Reuben, Simeon, Gad, Judah, Issachar, Zebulun, Ephraim, Manasseh, Benjamin, Dan, Asher, Naphtali. The only difference between this order and that of Num. 2 is in the position of the tribes of Reuben, Simeon and Gad – the camp of Reuben. Apart from this the lists are identical. Why the list of Num. 2 should give the order which does appear there is not very clear, but it may be[6] that the camps of Ephraim and Dan are located according to their geographical position in the land, that the camp of Judah is given by the priestly author the place of honour in the east and at the head of the list, and that the camp of Reuben is assigned the only other place remaining in the south. This does not necessarily mean that Num. 1.20–43 in its present form is the original list from which the order of Num. 2 is derived; it simply means that Num. 1.20–43 and Num. 2 present basically the same form of list.

Apart from Num. 1.5–15 and Num. 26, the only other list of this second group which omits Levi is to be found in Num. 13, where the order of tribes is: Reuben, Simeon, Judah, Issachar, Ephraim Benjamin, Zebulun, Manasseh, Dan, Asher, Naphtali and Gad. However, the text here has been disrupted, and for this reason and because of the occurrence of a Persian name in v. 14,[7] this list can safely be left out of consideration as a relatively late construction. So the question which remains to be decided in connection with those lists which omit Levi concerns the relationship of the lists to be found in Num. 1.5–15; Num. 26 and the list basic to Num. 2 and Num. 1.20–43.

The order of the tribes in Num. 1.5–15 is: Reuben, Simeon, Judah, Issachar, Zebulun, Ephraim, Manasseh, Benjamin, Dan, Asher, Gad, Naphtali; while in Num. 26.5–51 the following order appears: Reuben, Simeon, Gad, Judah, Issachar, Zebulun, Manasseh, Ephraim, Benjamin, Dan, Asher, Naphtali. At first sight the list of Num. 26, in view of the position of the tribe of Gad, bears a closer relationship to the list basic to Num. 1.20–43 and Num. 2 than does the list of Num. 1.5–15. The only difference is that in Num. 26 the order of the sons of Joseph is Manasseh-Ephraim, while in the list of Num. 1.20–43 and Num. 2 the order given is Ephraim-Manasseh. However, according to Noth,[8] the order in which the sons of Joseph appear is significant. The old

J and E sources in Gen. 41.51–52; 48.1, 13–14, 17–19, 20b show an original precedence of Manasseh before Ephraim, while P apparently knows only the order Ephraim-Manasseh. Thus, it is argued that Num. 26 represents an independent tradition, while the list basic to Num. 1.20–43 and Num. 2 is in fact based on the list which appears in Num. 1.5–15 where the order Ephraim-Manasseh is found. In support of this there is the additional point that it is from Num. 1.5–15 that Num. 2 has taken the names of the heads of the tribes. But if the list basic to Num. 1.20–43 and Num. 2 is thus based on Num. 1.5–15, then it must be understood that originally in Num. 1.5–15 the tribe of Gad appeared after Simeon as in Num. 1.20–43 and Num. 2. This leaves Noth with two basic lists of the second group: Num. 1.5–15 (with Gad coming after Simeon) and Num. 26; and the priority is assigned to the list of Num. 26 since it preserves the original order of the sons of Joseph: Manasseh-Ephraim.[9]

However, this argument clearly has one very weak link. This lies in Noth's assumption that originally the list of Num. 1.5–15 had the tribe of Gad in third place and that this was subsequently changed. There is no indication that this is a justifiable assumption, and if it were true that the original form of Num. 1.5–15 had Gad in third place it is probable, if one considers the order of tribes in Num. 13, that any change would have resulted in Gad's appearing right at the end of the list, and not, as in Num. 1.5–15, between Asher and Naphtali. So we would accept the list of Num. 1.5–15 in its present order as the only form in which this particular list ever appeared. Thus, the question of the relationship of these lists is still open.

This leads to another point crucial to Noth's argument: can the order in which the sons of Joseph are given be used in order to argue that the list of Num. 26 must be given the priority over against that of Num. 1.5–15? It is true that in the JE narrative in Gen. 48 Manasseh is said to be the first-born son of Joseph. However, this item of information cannot be treated in isolation; it must be seen within its context, and this context includes Gen. 48.13–20 in which Jacob's blessing of the two sons of Joseph is described. According to these verses Ephraim received the blessing of the first-born which was due to Manasseh. That this, however, reflects an original precedence of Manasseh over Ephraim, whatever Noth may mean precisely by that, so that the list of Num. 26 is to be given priority over that of Num. 1.5–15 and thus to be dated earlier than the latter, cannot immediately be accepted. In the first place, and most important, it is impossible to establish that at any time in the period of the judges, and probably also later, did Manasseh attain a position of superiority over Ephraim which would of itself explain the place of Manasseh as the first-born son of Joseph in Gen. 48. Indeed, from what we know of the history of Manasseh such superiority is almost out of the question.[10]

If Manasseh's position as the first-born son of Joseph is not to be explained on the basis of historical circumstances, then it seems that the only alternative is to explain it from a literary point of view.[11] That this is, in fact, the correct procedure is confirmed by the fact that it goes a considerable way towards explaining the curious way in which Gen. 48.13–20 describes the blessing which Jacob imparted to the sons of Joseph. This story uses a particular narrative technique which has the effect that the greatness and significance of a person or tribe is enhanced through being set against a background in which that person or tribe stands at an initial disadvantage. Jacob is all the more significant a figure for being the son of a mother who was for a long time childless and for being the younger of the two sons born to her (Gen. 25.21ff.); no doubt the struggles and difficulties which he experienced, culminating in his wrestling with a divine antagonist at the Jabbok (Gen. 32.25ff. [EVV vv. 24ff.]), before being able to settle in the land of Palestine, should be seen in the same light. The stature of Joseph is increased by the same technique; his mother also had been barren (Gen. 29.31; 30.1f.), and it is in the first instance as the youngest son that the narrative dealing with Joseph in Egypt describes the difficulties and dangers he survived eventually to become lord over his brethren.[12] It is, therefore, in the light of this that the description of Manasseh as the first-born son must be seen. Ephraim is shown as the younger son simply in order to enhance his superior position. The story does not, therefore, depend on any original precedence of Manasseh over Ephraim; it simply uses the artistic technique of making Manasseh the foil to Ephraim's greatness, a technique which is apparent in other narratives.

This means, then, that those tribal lists which name Ephraim as the first of the sons of Joseph reflect the actual historical conditions, while Num. 26 follows the literary presentation of Gen. 48

in placing Manasseh before Ephraim. The latter order originated in narrative skill, and since it is present in both J and E it was probably also the order which appeared in the basis of these two Pentateuchal documents and so must be dated to a time before the composition of both of them.[13] Therefore, it cannot be argued on the basis of the order of appearance of the sons of Joseph that the list which puts Ephraim in first place is necessarily earlier than that which assigns this place to Manasseh. On the other hand, however, it is also clear that Noth can no longer be followed in using this argument in order to assign the priority to the list which gives Manasseh first place. Another basis must be found for determining which list has the priority.

Since the only other difference between these lists of the second group which omits Levi is in the place which is assigned to the tribe of Gad, it is here if anywhere that it will be possible to find reason for deciding the question of which of these lists is original and which presents a derived, secondary form.

It has already been noted that it is unlikely that in Num. 1.5–15 Gad originally appeared in third place. On the one hand, there is nothing which compels this assumption; and on the other hand, if the assumption were to be accepted, it is most probable that a subsequent change in the order of the tribes would have resulted in Gad's being placed at the end of the list where it appears in Num. 13. This constitutes a primary reason for understanding Num. 1.5–15 as the original form of the tribal list, and for taking as secondary that form of the list in which Gad appears in third place. Moreover, this conclusion is supported by the fact that it is possible to explain to some extent why at a later stage the tribe of Gad was transferred from its original position between Asher and Naphtali to the third place in the list, whereas it is not possible to give adequate reason for the assumption that in the original form of Num. 1.5–15 Gad stood in third place.

Noth accounted for the change in the position of the tribe of Gad in the following way: the first form of the system of twelve tribes has Levi in third position. This represents the original form of the system. However, in time this system was modified because of the disappearance of Levi as a 'secular' tribe, and the gap thus created in the group of tribes constituting the sons of Leah was filled by the transfer of the tribe of Gad, which, with the tribes of Dan, Asher and Naphtali, did not belong to a really fixed group of tribes, to the place formerly occupied by Levi. In this way there originated the second form of the tribal system which we meet, for example, in Num. 26. However, as we shall see later in connection with the discussion of the first group of tribal lists represented by Gen. 49, this view is wholly dependent on a particular interpretation of the saying about Levi in Gen. 49.5–7 which is not altogether certain. So, if possible, another way of accounting for the position of Gad should be sought.

The explanation seems to lie in fact within the context of P itself where these lists of the second group have their present framework,[14] and more specifically in the context of the list basic to Num. 1.20–43 and Num. 2. The former passage deals with the numbering of those able to go to war, and the latter with the actual lay-out of the camp. So the passages, besides being based on a similar tribal list, are related also in the subject with which they deal. It is this subject which provides the clue to the place which the tribe of Gad occupies. According to Num. 2, the camp was divided into four companies, each company being placed at one of the four points of the compass and consisting of three tribes. The name given to each company is that of the first named of the three tribes. Thus, the company consisting of Reuben, Simeon and Gad is called Reuben, while that consisting of Judah, Issachar and Zebulun is called Judah, and so on. If it is assumed for the moment that the tribal list of Num. 1.5–15 represents the original and basic list of those lists belonging to the second group, then it can readily be appreciated why the tribe of Gad was transferred to third place. The division of the tribes into their separate camps would, following the order of tribes in Num. 1.5–15, have resulted in Judah's being included in the camp bearing the name of Reuben. Such a situation would not have been tolerated by the priestly writer. It was for this reason, to obviate the chance of Judah's being placed in an inferior position, that it was found necessary to complete the camp of Reuben with a tribe other than Judah. Why it was that the tribe of Gad in particular was chosen for this is not so clear, but since this is a problem inherent also in Noth's view it cannot really be used as an argument against the view put forward here and in favour of that of Noth. It can only be tentatively suggested that historical circumstances connected Gad with Reuben and thus led to the inclusion of Gad within the camp of Reuben.[15]

On the basis of the foregoing, then, the following conclusion can be drawn: the basic and original list of tribes within that group which does not include Levi is to be found in Num. 1.5–15. From this list there was derived first of all that list which is basic to Num. 2.3–31; 7.12–83; 10.14–28 and to Num. 1.20–43. Numbers 2.3–31 derived the names of the leaders of each tribe from the already existing Num. 1.5–15, but the order of the tribes given in this derived list, with Gad in third place, came about when the list was used to describe the plan of the camp. The order of the sons of Joseph, with Ephraim first, as given in the original list, was retained for the derived list also. It was then at a later stage still that the list of Num. 26 originated. Following the pattern set by the list of Num. 1.20–43 and Num. 2, the position of the tribe of Gad in the third place was retained. However, because of the order of the sons of Joseph given in Gen. 48, which we have already seen to be based on a narrative technique, Num. 26 put Manasseh before Ephraim.[16] Then, at a final stage in the history of this group of lists, there comes the list of Num. 13 where the tribe of Gad has been taken from its secondary position as third tribe and put at the end of the list. Num. 1.5–15 must, therefore, be taken as the original and basic form of the tribal lists of this group.

With the tribal lists of the first group which includes Levi, the problems are somewhat different. There are two such lists to be considered: Gen. 49.3–27 and Gen. 29.31–30.24. In the former the order in which the tribes appear is: Reuben, Simeon, Levi, Judah, Zebulun, Issachar, Dan, Gad, Asher, Naphtali, Joseph, Benjamin. In the latter the order is: Reuben, Simeon, Levi, Judah, Dan, Naphtali, Gad, Asher, Issachar, Zebulun, Joseph, (Benjamin).[17] Other lists of this group are to be found in Gen. 35.23f.; 46.8–24; Ex. 1.2ff.; Deut. 27.12f.; I Chron. 2.1f. and Ezek. 48.31ff. However, all of these, with the probable exception of the last mentioned,[18] should most likely be taken as dependent on Gen. 29–30. This is clear from the order in which the tribes appear: in some cases with Issachar and Zebulun, in that order, separated from Reuben, Simeon, Levi and Judah; in the remaining lists with these six tribes together; in all cases with Dan-Naphtali together and Gad-Asher together.[19] Although all four of these tribes are not always found together, yet the association of Dan with Naphtali and of Gad with Asher connects these lists with Gen. 29–30 rather than with Gen. 49. This, in effect, leaves us with two basic lists of this group: Gen. 29–30 and Gen. 49. These two lists are similar in many respects, but they also display two important differences: in the first place, the tribes of Issachar and Zebulun are in reverse order in Gen. 49; secondly, the succession Dan, Naphtali, Gad, Asher, appears in Gen. 49 as Dan, Gad, Asher, Naphtali.

How these differences are to be explained, and how it is to be decided which represents the original order in this group of lists are difficult and uncertain questions. There is no compelling reason for the view that Zebulun-Issachar is the original order which was changed for no apparent reason by E.[20] On the other hand, there is nothing to indicate that Issachar-Zebulun was the original order which then was changed by the compiler of Gen. 49. However, it is possible to argue that the order in which the 'concubine' tribes are given in Gen. 29–30 was dictated, on the one hand, by the fact that the tribes of Dan and Naphtali occupied adjacent territory in Palestine, and, on the other hand, by the similarity in content of the popular etymologies given to the tribes of Gad and Asher. In this way the conclusion could be reached that the order of Gen. 49 is the original which was then changed, for the reasons just given, by the compiler of Gen. 29–30. This is a possible course to adopt, but the chances of its being the correct one are somewhat diminished by another consideration. For this, reference must be made to the place of Joseph and Benjamin in the lists. In both lists they are to be found right at the end. There is nothing in Gen. 49 which would account for this. Genesis 29–30 does, however, provide an explanation.[21] The aim of this narrative is clearly the birth of Joseph. The motif of the loved and unloved wives of Jacob, Rachel's long period of childlessness during which Leah bore six sons to Jacob, all must be seen as having their culminating point in the birth of Joseph to Rachel. Just as with the stories dealing with Jacob, with Joseph in Egypt, and with Jacob's blessing of the sons of Joseph,[22] so also here a narrative technique is used with the aim of exalting a particular individual.[23] This well accounts for the place of Joseph at the end of the list of the sons of Jacob, and it may be for this reason that Joseph and Benjamin come at the end of the list of tribes in Gen. 49 also. Following this argument then, the list of Gen. 29–30 would have to be taken as the original form of this group of tribal lists.

In the light of this it is clear that no certain conclusion can be drawn at the moment on the question of which of these two lists represents the original form in this group. Fortunately, however, this uncertainty does not hinder our passing on to deal with further questions in connection with these lists, for in spite of their differences the lists of Gen. 29–30 and Gen. 49 are basically similar; at least they are similar in those respects which are of direct concern here. Among the twelve sons of Jacob they distinguish three groups: the first group consists of Reuben, Simeon, Levi, Judah, Issachar and Zebulun; the second of Dan, Naphtali, Gad and Asher; and the third of Joseph and Benjamin. Our next problem, then concerns the relative ages of this list and that to be found in Num. 1.5–15.

The main difference between these lists, on which the question of their relative ages hinges, concerns the tribe of Levi. Noth's view that the list which includes Levi is earlier than that in which Levi does not appear is based on the argument that it is easier to explain how Levi came to be omitted from the list than it is to account for Levi as a late-comer into the list of tribes. This, in turn, depends on the view that in Gen. 49.5–7 Levi is spoken of as a 'secular' tribe, for it is only with such an understanding that Levi's subsequent absence from the list can be explained.[24] So our primary question must then be: is Levi in Gen. 49.5–7 a 'secular' tribe just as the other tribes? The passage refers to the scattering of Simeon and Levi throughout Israel, which will take place because of the anger and violence of these tribes. The passage, in fact, presupposes that Simeon and Levi *are* scattered, they possess no land like the other tribes; and in order to explain this state of affairs reference is made to an event in the past in which these tribes played such a dishonourable part that their being divided and scattered was the promised consequence.[25] The event to which reference is made is most probably that described in Gen. 34. According to this tradition, Simeon and Levi, against the will of their father Jacob, made an attack on Shechem because of the rape of their sister Dinah. Since Simeon and Levi are shown acting together, and since the event described coincides well enough with the anger and violence of Simeon and Levi in Gen. 49.5–7, it may then be understood that the tradition of Gen. 34 forms the background to the saying on Simeon and Levi in Gen. 49. In Gen. 34 there is no indication of the priestly status of Levi; the tribe is simply one among the others and so may be taken as a 'secular' tribe.[26] However, because Levi is a secular tribe in Gen. 34 it does not necessarily follow that the same is true of Levi in Gen.

49.5–7. The latter passage simply presupposes that Simeon and Levi possess no land in Israel, and to explain this the passage refers to an already existing tradition now preserved in Gen. 34. Moreover, one could go further than this. There is no indication in Gen. 34 that as a result of their attack on Shechem Simeon and Levi were scattered throughout Israel. Apart from the fact that by this action these tribes earned their father's condemnation, it is, according to the tradition (Gen. 34.30), Jacob and his whole family who have been endangered by Simeon and Levi. The composer of Gen. 49.5–7 can, therefore, be argued to have drawn an unwarranted conclusion by connecting the landless status of Simeon and Levi with the event handed down in the tradition of Gen. 34. Because the reference to the tradition of Gen. 34 can be taken simply as aetiological with no historical foundation, and because it is known that the *priestly* tribe of Levi possessed no land among the rest of the tribes,[27] it could indeed be concluded that Gen. 49.5–7 refers not to the secular but to the priestly tribe of Levi.[28]

However, this argument is not conclusive. Levi in Gen. 49 is simply presupposed as being without land of its own. If this state was the historical result of the event described in Gen. 34 then the Levi of Gen. 49 would probably also be a secular tribe. However, even though such a historical connection probably does not exist, it does not follow that the Levi of Gen. 49 must be the priestly tribe. Genesis 34 is not the only tradition in which Levi is presented as a non-priestly group. In Judg. 17–18 the Levite is only a priest by virtue of the fact that he has been instituted as such by Micah the Ephraimite.[29] Priesthood was a function to which a man, not necessarily but perhaps preferably a Levite in the period of the judges, was instituted. It was not a state to which all Levites belonged simply by virtue of their being Levites, at least in the early period. The Levite of Judg. 17 was not a priest before he was instituted by Micah; rather, like the Levite of Judg. 19.1ff., he was a 'resident alien' (*gēr*)[30] who had formerly resided in Judah but now had left that territory. It may be to a group of such landless, non-priestly Levites that reference is made in Gen. 49.5–7. While the fact that no priestly functions of the Levites are indicated in Gen. 49 may be taken in support of this interpretation, it should nevertheless be realized that Deut. 33.11 makes clear that even the priestly Levites were not without enemies who would be capable of pronouncing such a curse on Levi as is to be found in Gen. 49.

It is, therefore, quite impossible at the present state of our knowledge to give a certain decision on whether Levi in Gen. 49 is the
secular or the priestly tribe.

That this is so is particularly unfortunate since the relative dating of the tribal lists depends to a large extent on the answer to this
question. If, on the one hand, it is understood that Gen. 49 refers
to the priestly tribe of Levi, then the only way of explaining the
absence of Levi in the tribal lists of the second group would be by
arguing that this latter form of the list derives from a period before
Levi had established itself as a priestly tribe; that is, the tribal list
from which Levi is absent would be based on a conception of the
constituent tribes of Israel earlier than that on which the list which
includes Levi is based. Once Levi as a priestly tribe had been included among the tribes of Israel there would certainly have been
no reason for its later omission. Furthermore, if it is then asked
why the tribe of Levi, as a late-comer into the tribal list, should
have been assigned the third place in the succession of tribes, this
could be explained by saying that because the composer of Gen.
49.5–7 used the tradition of Gen. 34 to explain the landless status
of Levi, he was compelled to follow that tradition and deal with
Simeon and Levi together.[31] Simeon already occupied second
place in the tribal list which did not have Levi, and so the inclusion of Levi meant that that tribe had to appear in third place.

On the other hand, if Levi in Gen. 49.5–7 is taken as the secular
tribe there is quite a different result for the relative dating of the
basic lists of these two groups. There would have been no grounds
for bringing Levi as a secular tribe into the list of tribes at a time
after there had already come into existence a selection of Isarelite
tribes in which Levi was not included. If Levi in Gen. 49 is a
secular tribe then the probability is that Noth is right in taking this
as an earlier selection of Israelite tribes than that represented by
those lists in which Levi does not appear. It could be argued, then,
that Levi was eventually omitted from the tribal list because there
no longer existed a secular group of Levites.

Since the relative date of these lists is uncertain, it is clearly also
quite impossible to be precise on the question of their absolute
dating. However, some general points may nevertheless be made.
Noth was able to date the list of Num. 26, which he took to be the
basic list of that group in which Levi does not appear, to the
second half of the period of the judges on the basis of the fact that

so few Canaanite city-states are mentioned in the list; the list must derive, therefore, from a time before these city-states had been absorbed into Israel. However, apart from the fact that in making so little reference to the Canaanite city-states the list preserves old tradition just at this one point, but does not necessarily itself derive from very early time,[32] this list of Num. 26 is not the basic one of the group of tribal lists which omit Levi. The basic list of this group is to be found in Num. 1.5–15, and here there is no such indication of the time of origin of the list. The event which is commemorated in the Song of Deborah in Judg. 5 forms a *terminus a quo*, for at this time the tribe of Manasseh had still not appeared, whereas this tribe is mentioned in Num. 1.5–15. On the other hand, the earliest *terminus ad quem* which can be fixed is probably the fall of the northern kingdom in 722/1 BC.

As for the tribal lists in which Levi appears, in Gen. 29.31–30.24 and Gen. 49.3–27, both of these, in their present form, may be dated to about the time of Solomon. Since both J and E in Gen. 29–30 contain this list it may be assumed that the list was present also in the common basis of these documents; but exactly how far back this brings the list is a matter for little more than speculation. With Gen. 49 it is difficult to arrive at any more certain conclusion. The problems here are somewhat different from those of the other lists since Gen. 49 is composed of what were originally independent sayings on the individual tribes.[33] This is clear from the fact that the sayings are not all cast in the same form; some of them, such as those on Zebulun and Issachar, deal with the tribes as such, while others, such as that on Reuben, personify the tribes in their eponyms. Further, there are two independent sayings about the tribe of Dan. However, that the collector of these sayings invented the order in which they are now presented is unlikely; it is much more probable that he based the order of the sayings on an order of the tribes which was already known. Thus, even if it is true that, for example, the saying about the tribe of Judah belongs to the period during which David was king over Judah in Hebron,[34] this is of no help in assigning a time of origin to the arrangement of tribes presupposed by the list as a whole. This arrangement could belong either before or after the time of origin of the individual sayings.

There is, however, one point which has been held to show an early origin for this type of list which includes Levi. The other feature of this type of list is that Joseph appears in it, whereas the lists of the other group have Ephraim and Manasseh. Noth argued[35] that Joseph is the original entity, while Ephraim and Manasseh are the two tribes into which this entity was divided after settlement in Palestine. Thus, support was found for dating the list of Gen. 49 before that of the second group, and, since Joseph does not appear in the Song of Deborah while Ephraim does, for dating the list of Gen. 49 to the first half of the period of the judges. However, while the simplicity of this view recommends it, it does conceal several serious difficulties which would, in fact, support the opposite point of view that the use of Joseph as a tribal name presupposes the earlier use of Ephraim and Manasseh as tribal names, so that Joseph would then be a collective designation for these two groups.[36]

The main difficulty of Noth's view is that Ephraim appears in the Song of Deborah whereas Manasseh does not. If Joseph was the original entity which later split into Ephraim and Manasseh, the absence of Manasseh from the Song of Deborah in Judg. 5 is strange. However, while no reference is made here to Manasseh, a tribe called Machir does appear; but it is very unlikely that Machir, which appears as an independent tribe in the Song of Deborah, was originally considered a full brother of Ephraim and son of Joseph. Machir is not associated with Ephraim in this way in the Song of Deborah, that is, at a time before the appearance of Manasseh as the brother of Ephraim. In other passages, however, where Machir and Manasseh are mentioned together, a different picture emerges. In Num. 26.29; 27.1 for example, Machir is the son of Manasseh and the father of Gilead. These passages presuppose that Machir was occupying the land of Gilead in east Jordan. But since, on the other hand, Gilead appears independently of Machir in the Song of Deborah, it must be understood that at the time of the event celebrated in the Song of Deborah Machir had not yet taken up residence in Gilead but was probably living in west Jordan.[37] Clearly, these passages reflect different stages of tribal movements and developments, and any reconstruction of the background events must be tentative. However, in the light of what we have said so far, together with the description of the area occupied by Joseph in Josh. 16–17, the following seems to be the most likely course of events which led to Machir's becoming the father of Gilead and the son of Manasseh:[38] at a time after the event commemorated in the Song of Deborah, when Philistine pressure was brought to bear on the mid-Palestinian tribes,[39] a part of the tribe of Ephraim was forced to migrate northwards into territory occupied by the independent tribe of Machir. While a certain amount of intermingling of Ephraimites and Machirites may then have taken place, the pressure exerted by these Ephraimites brought about the migration of most of Machir to east Jordan where the tribe is found from this time on. Meanwhile, those left behind in the territory formerly inhabited by Machir formed themselves into a tribe independent of, yet related to, both Ephraim and Machir. This new tribe called itself Manasseh, perhaps after the name of its leading family or after an ancestor.[40] Then, at a later stage, the relationship of these tribes was fixed genealogically by making Ephraim and Manasseh full brothers and sons of Joseph, and Machir the son of Manasseh. Manasseh, though a new tribe, became the 'father' of Machir probably simply because it occupied a part of the more significant west Jordan while Machir settled in the less important east Jordan. This reconstruction accounts for (1) the appearance of Ephraim and Machir as independent tribes in the Song of Deborah, and the absence of Manasseh, (2) the appearance of Machir as living at one time in west Jordan and at another time in east Jordan, (3) Machir's direct relationship to Gilead and to Manasseh, and his indirect relationship to Ephraim and to Joseph.

It is most unlikely that the name Joseph was ever used simply as an alternative to the name Ephraim,[41] and there is no evidence that Joseph was the original group which later divided into Ephraim and Machir; yet, in the light of what we have said, one of these views must be adopted if Joseph is to be accepted as the original entity. It would seem, therefore, that as a tribal name Joseph is a collective designation which came into use only after the tribal movements and the stabilization of tribal relationships, as described above, which resulted in the emergence of Manasseh as a 'brother'-tribe to Ephraim.[42] However, this conclusion does not necessarily mean that the list of Gen. 49, which includes Joseph, is later than the list of Num. 1.5–15, which has Ephraim and Manasseh rather than Joseph. Undoubtedly, Ephraim and Manasseh could be considered for a long period either as two groups bearing those names or as one group called Joseph. In the context of the tribal lists the decision on how these tribes should be designated depended on how many other tribes were to be

included in the lists. In other words, the inclusion or omission of
Levi was the primary consideration, and so also it remains the
crucial point in the question of the relative dating of the tribal
lists. On the other hand, however, if it is true, as we have argued,
that the use of the designation Joseph as a tribal name presupposes
the existence of Ephraim and Manasseh, then the tribal list of Gen.
49 must, like that of Num. 1.5–15, come from a time after the event
which is celebrated in the Song of Deborah.

This conclusion is supported by a further point. Our concern is
with the tribe of Gad. Gad is mentioned in the lists belonging to
both groups, but does not appear in the Song of Deborah. Here,
however, the name Gilead is found. Although Gilead is normally
a district name, it is unlikely that this is its significance in the context of the Song of Deborah[43] where otherwise it is tribes to which
reference is made.[44] Gilead must, therefore, be taken here as a
tribal name, used with reference to those inhabiting that area of
east Jordan. On the other hand, Gilead is not to be identified with
Gad.[45] Although the latter is not mentioned in the Song of
Deborah, and although Gilead is not found otherwise as a tribal
name, this cannot be taken to indicate that Gilead means Gad in
the Song of Deborah. The description of east Jordan in I Sam. 13.7
as the land of Gad and Gilead is accurate in so far as it implies that
Gad and Gilead were separate parts of east Jordan. This corresponds with the early list of place names in Num. 32.34–38, given
as a description of the area occupied by Reuben and Gad, in that
this comprises the area lying precisely outside Gilead. Gilead
itself, according to Num. 32.39–42, was the area eventually settled
by Machir. Gad, therefore, remains completely unnoticed in the
Song of Deborah.

The aim of the author of the central section of the Song of
Deborah, with which we are concerned here,[46] is to praise those
tribes which took part in the battle against Sisera and to reprimand
those which did not take part. But the inevitable effect of this was
that the author referred to every Israelite tribe which in his opinion
could and should have participated. Only by such an understanding is it possible to explain why some tribes are reprimanded.
There are five Israelite tribes, however, which appear in the tribal
lists but which are not mentioned in the Song of Deborah. These
are Manasseh, Judah, Simeon, Levi and Gad. The tribe of
Manasseh we have just dealt with; the absence of Levi could be

explained on the basis of the supposition that as a landless and/or priestly tribe it could not have been expected to participate; the historical circumstances which would have prevented the participation of Judah and Simeon will be our concern at a later stage.[47] Similar historical circumstances which might explain the absence of Gad are, however, impossible to find. It cannot be argued that the event commemorated here was the concern only of the mid-Palestinian and Galilean tribes, so that Gad, as a tribe settled in east Jordan, would not have been expected to be present. Gad, according to the information available, was settled in east Jordan beside Gilead, and Gilead is referred to in the Song of Deborah. The inevitable conclusion, then, is that at the time of the event commemorated in the Song of Deborah there existed no Israelite tribe of Gad.[48] If this is the case, then both types of tribal list must come from a time after the battle against Sisera celebrated in the Song of Deborah.

To sum up this section: Num. 1.5–15 represents the original tribal list from which are derived those other lists of the group which does not include Levi. Since it includes the tribes of Manasseh and Gad it must come from a time later than the battle against Sisera celebrated in the Song of Deborah. While the date of this list relative to the list which includes Levi cannot be established with any certainty, mainly because the Levi of Gen. 49.5–7 could be either the priestly or the secular tribe, this latter list must also be dated to a time after the battle against Sisera because of the occurrence in the list of the tribes of Joseph and Gad. The lists of both groups have the common aim of preserving the number twelve of the Israelite tribes, while the chief differences between them are due to the inclusion or omission of Levi.[49]

Thus, if an amphictyony ever existed, that is, if there ever was such a federation of Israelite tribes corresponding to either or both of the groups of lists, arranged in the way which Noth has described, it must have existed in the period between the battle against Sisera and the rise of the monarchy. However, this is only the case if the proposed Israelite amphictyony must correspond to the lists of tribes. If the Israelite amphictyony was composed of members which did not exactly correspond to the tribes mentioned in the lists then these lists are in large measure irrelevant to the whole question. In fact, it has been argued, even by Noth himself,[50] that not all twelve of the Israelite tribes enjoyed contemporaneous, independent existence at any particular time; that is to say, it seems that it is impossible to point to any period and say that in that particular period there were twelve co-existing, independent Israelite tribes corresponding to the tribal lists. For example, Reuben and Simeon, in the period of which we are comparatively well informed, play no significant role. They are assigned no independent territory in the original border lists along with the other tribes,[51] and it is probably their debilitated state which is presupposed in the curses they receive in the so-called blessing of Jacob in Gen. 49.3ff. It is impossible to plot accurately the course of the history of each individual tribe; however, since both Josh. 19.1ff. and Judg. 1.2f. reflect conditions in which there were only a few Simeonites living within the territory of Judah, there is reason for believing that the decline of Simeon started at a very early time. Reuben is mentioned in the Song of Deborah in Judg. 5.15f., but other references indicate that all that remained of this tribe amounted to a few families, some perhaps absorbed into the tribe of Judah, though claiming to be Reubenite, while others seem to have settled in Transjordan.[52] Furthermore, the tribe of Dan, even if it remained independent, was of little significance.[53] And, finally, it is difficult to see how a landless group like the Levites could have fitted into the scheme of each tribe maintaining a central sanctuary for a month in the year.

If this is true it seriously weakens the case for the existence of an amphictyony in Israel, especially if it is the numerical aspect of the comparison between the Greek and Hebrew tribal organizations, that is, their common use of the number twelve or multiples of it, which is taken to be the essential factor. However, according to Noth,[54] this is not necessarily the case. His argument, if I understand it correctly, is that just because the number twelve, as this is consistently preserved in the lists, appears to be unreliably schematic, the general historicity of the system of twelve tribes as an actual institution is not thereby disproved. Often enough in the course of history use has been made of a given historical situation as the raw material on which to erect institutions and organizations. An example of this is the division of the kingdom by Solomon into twelve administrative districts, a division which was made for purely practical purposes. The historical reality of this administrative institution is not doubted even though the distrusted number twelve is basic to it, and the reason for this is that we are well informed about the aims for which the institution was established.

The implication of this argument is presumably this: because, for example, the tribe of Simeon was a weak tribe in the period of the judges and probably was unable to maintain an independent existence, this does not disprove the existence of the amphictyony as an institution of twelve tribes with Simeon as one of its members. The nominal membership of the amphictyony is one thing, but the practical membership, in terms of the duties of each member with regard especially to the central sanctuary, is quite another. So, then, before the amphictyony theory can be disproved it has to be shown that the presence of a particular institution as the basis of the system is historically impossible.

However, apart from the fact that the existence of the amphictyony must be proved and not just disproved, the rest of the argument cannot be followed. It is perfectly true that institutions and organizations are erected on raw material and also that Solomon's division of the kingdom is a good example of this. But that the latter is a good analogy for the situation in the period of the judges is highly questionable. Solomon's twelve districts were not named after, nor did their territorial extent coincide with the areas occupied by, the tribes. Furthermore, Solomon's division of the kingdom presupposed the existence of a people Israel with a centralized authority. On the other hand, according to Noth's theory, the people Israel originated on the soil of Palestine on the basis of the amphictyonic connection of the tribes. If the analogy with Solomon's division of the kingdom were to hold good, one would have to understand that this people called Israel already existed before the setting up of the amphictyony. For only by such an understanding would it be possible to explain how an institution with twelve members, all of which had practical duties, could be erected on raw material consisting of less than twelve active and independent tribes. Also in this hypothetical case the divisions would have to disregard in some measure the individual units represented by the individual tribes. Noth's analogy presupposes the existence of the people Israel with a centralized authority as something earlier than the amphictyony.

However, this argument against Noth is really valid only if it is true that the members of an amphictyony had to be twelve or a multiple of that number. But it has to be recognized that the numbers six and twelve are not the only basis of federations within the Old Testament itself as well as in Greece and Italy. In the Old

Testament there is the federation of the five cities of the Philistines;[55] the coalition of five kings in Gen. 14; the five kings of Midian in Num. 31.8; the five kings of the Amorites in Josh. 10.5; the five sons of Judah in I Chron. 2.4; and the four cities of the Gibeonites in Josh. 9.17. It is out of the question, of course, that all these should be claimed as amphictyonies, but on the other hand it is clear that the Greek and Italian amphictyonies did not always consist of six or twelve members.[56] The number twelve is particularly associated with the idea of an amphictyony on account of the importance placed on the league at Delphi about which we have more information than any other. However, in the Kalaurian league there were seven members (Strabo 8.6.14), while the Lykian league was made up of twenty-three cities. In Thucydides IV, 91, reference is made to eleven Boeotarchs who appear to have been the civil and military leaders of the cities and the league.[57]

Thus, the numbers of tribes reckoned as Israelite in the tribal lists is not in itself sufficient reason either for assuming or for denying the existence of an Israelite amphictyony. The other evidence which has been adduced in favour of the existence of an amphictyony must, therefore, be examined.

B. *The Central Sanctuary*

The essential characteristic of the amphictyonies, at least as they were organized in Greece, was the central sanctuary, the sanctuary which the individual members of the amphictyony were obligated to support and defend. Here matters of common concern were discussed and for this purpose each amphictyonic member had its representative; in Israel, it is argued,[58] this representative bore the title *nāśī'*. As well as being used in this way, however, the central sanctuary was also the place where common acts of worship took place. At the Israelite central sanctuary this common worship had the form of regular festivals at which the covenant between Israel and its God Yahweh was periodically renewed. This covenant ceremony was the concrete expression of the allegiance of all the tribes to Yahweh. It should also be understood, therefore, that at the central sanctuary Israel's most important cult object, the ark, was deposited. While there is some dispute among the advocates of the theory of the Israelite amphictyony as to which of the Israelite sanctuaries functioned as the central sanctuary, in Noth's

view this position was occupied in the first instance by the sanctuary at Shechem; at a later stage, however, the ark was moved
from Shechem and, following its movements, one may conclude
that Shechem was replaced as central sanctuary by Bethel, then
Bethel by Gilgal, while the latter was in time succeeded by Shiloh
where the ark was to be found at the end of the period of the
judges.[59]

In order that a sanctuary should qualify as the central sanctuary
of the old Israelite amphictyony it must, therefore, fulfil three
requirements: there should be evidence that the sanctuary was
acknowledged and visited by all the tribes or their representatives;
the festival of covenant renewal must have been celebrated there;
and it must be shown that the ark was lodged at that particular
sanctuary during the period in which it is supposed to have been
the central sanctuary.[60]

However, when the records connected with and deriving from
the various sanctuaries proposed as central sanctuaries are examined with these criteria in mind, it is clear that none of them show
unequivocally that any of these sanctuaries was a central sanctuary.
This is the case even with Shechem, where the amphictyony is
supposed to have been founded at the entry of the house of Joseph
under Joshua and which is thus the most likely candidate for the
position of central sanctuary.

One of the most important sources for Shechem is Josh. 24.
However, its significance is far from being beyond dispute. Even
its position, coming after Josh. 23, is a matter for discussion, for it
is clearly the latter chapter which constitutes the deuteronomistic
conclusion to the history of the conquest of Palestine. Joshua 23,
where Joshua is an old man about to die (v. 14), and which therefore is hardly a suitable prelude to Josh. 24, finds its continuation
in the deuteronomistic historical work in Judg. 2.6ff.[61] However,
since Josh. 24 itself shows signs of deuteronomistic editing,[62]
it must be understood that this chapter is a separate tradition which
has been introduced into its present position by a secondary
deuteronomistic redaction.

While this makes it extremely unlikely that either J or E (or
both) is present in Josh. 24,[63] it does not necessarily mean that old
tradition is also absent from this chapter. Joshua 24 has certainly
undergone deuteronomistic editing on an extensive scale, but the
whole chapter cannot thereby be dismissed as little more than a

pious sermon by someone steeped in covenant ideas and terminology.

Joshua 24 purports to be the record of a historical act in which the Israelite tribes, at the challenge of Joshua, affirmed their acceptance of the worship of Yahweh. However, it has been felt that to accept the chapter simply for what it says raises the difficulty that according to the tradition of Ex. 19–24 the people of Israel had long before at Sinai become worshippers of Yahweh. How is it that it is only now that they are asked to put away the foreign gods and serve Yahweh, and how is it that it is only now that they receive the statute and ordinance which, according to the tradition, they had long ago received at Sinai? To solve these questions it has been proposed that what we find predicated of all Israel in Ex. 19–24 and Josh. 24 really concerned only a part of the people, and that in fact it was only Joshua and his house, that is, the Rachel tribes, which had experienced Egypt and the Exodus and were now introducing the worship of Yahweh to tribes already long settled in the land.[64]

This solution is, however, open to serious question.[65] A contrast is certainly drawn in Josh. 24 between the house of Joshua and the rest of the people, but if the simple expedient is adopted of accepting this as historical, then one cannot dismiss as unhistorical the reply of the people to the choice set before them by Joshua (v. 16): 'far be it from us to forsake Yahweh to serve other gods'. This presupposes that the people were already worshippers of Yahweh. Furthermore, in the context of the solution which has been put forward, the choice offered by Joshua makes no sense. Joshua, according to the theory, was not the leader of the people whom he was addressing; these people had long ago entered the land and so would have had behind them the decision on which gods they were to worship. In fact, there is nothing in Josh. 24 dealing with the union of different tribal groups, for both the house of Joshua and those addressed by Joshua were already united in the worship of Yahweh. In effect, Joshua is here challenging the people to re-affirm their acceptance of the worship of Yahweh, and to this end he and his house provide the lead.

If this is correct, if there is nothing here about the union of independent tribal groups which would have demanded as background the period immediately after settlement in the land, then the whole question of the historical background of this chapter is open once more. It has been in the hope of finding this background that it has been argued that 24.1–28 correspond in form with the Hittite vassal treaties, of which the latest belongs to the thirteenth century BC, and so Josh. 24 has been taken to reflect covenant practice in Israel at a very early age.[66] However, even if the parallel between the Hittite treaties and Josh. 24 can stand, which is very doubtful, it is clearly quite impossible to draw any sure historical conclusions from this form-critical observation.[67] It is only on the basis of an examination of Josh. 24 within the Israelite and Old Testament context that any safe conclusions will be drawn as far as the historical background of what is recorded here is concerned.

We noted earlier that Josh. 24 has undergone deuteronomistic editing. That this is editing, rather than simply composition, is clear from the fact that old elements probably are to be found in the chapter. Nevertheless, since the hand of the deuteronomist is quite evident, it is from his point of time and his point of view that we must enquire after possible ancient elements within the chapter.

In this connection, reference has been made to 24.2–13,[68] which give a historical review of Yahweh's dealings with his people up to and including the conquest of the land. It has been noted that in form these verses present an extended version of what is to be found in Deut. 6.20–24; 26.5–9. The last mentioned of these passages in particular has been understood to reveal what in fact the form is: it is a creed, and the statements of faith which it contains form the basis of the presentation of Israel's history which is to be found in the Pentateuch. However, even if Deut. 26.5–9 is to be seen as an early creed,[69] it does not follow that the same is the case with Josh. 24.2–13. In the first place, while the form of these two passages may be basically similar, their purpose is not. The latter is not a creed; if a creed is to be found in Josh. 24 it is in vv. 16f. Secondly, rather than that Josh. 24.2–13 should form the basis of the Pentateuchal account of Israel's history, it is much more likely that it is in fact a summary of that history and presupposes the Pentateuchal presentation. It is clear that vv. 2–4, at any rate, presuppose a time when the different patriarchal traditions had been brought together and when the patriarchs themselves had been arranged in the chronological order in which they are now to be found in the Pentateuch.[70]

The historical review leads up to the invitation by Joshua that the people should choose which god they wished to serve. It has been argued[71] that this invitation would find its best context in the period immediately after the conquest when there would have been the question of accepting the worship of the deities of the newly won land or of maintaining and re-interpreting the religion of Yahweh, the God from Sinai. However, while this is possible, it is not really satisfactory since it does not account for the reference to the 'gods whom your fathers served beyond the river', i.e. the gods of Mesopotamia. In fact this latter feature of the chapter would find a better background in the late monarchy period, when Israel was under the domination of Assyria, or even the exilic period when Babylon was Israel's oppressor, for at this time the problem of maintaining the worship of Yahweh over against the Canaanite gods on the one hand and the Mesopotamian gods on the other was really one of pressing concern.[72] It may be this concern and this background which are reflected in Josh. 24.14ff.

But Josh. 24.14ff. belong closely with what precedes. The historical review leads up to the demand which follows.[73] Moreover, the worship of the gods of Mesopotamia also figures in that review. The first eighteen verses of the chapter should, then, be seen as a unit. Since this whole section, therefore, presupposes the Pentateuchal presentation of history, would find a good background in the late monarchy or exilic period, and has deuteronomistic language at many points, it is most probable that we should treat it as a deuteronomistic composition. In spite of this, however, it is possible that in one respect the section does reflect ancient practice. Connected with Joshua's invitation there is the summons to put away the foreign gods, and it is precisely here that there may be a reflection of ancient cultic practice at Shechem. There is reference to such a ritual in Gen. 35.2ff.[74] where again it is connected with Shechem and, although its origin is quite obscure,[75] it is certainly possible that it was an ancient rite, associated with Shechem and taken over into Israelite religion and used as a symbolic gesture of renunciation of pagan cults and obedience to Yahweh.[76]

The next section of the chapter in vv. 19–24 is, however, late.[77] The statement 'you cannot serve Yahweh' is strange coming after vv. 14ff.; there is a good deal of repetition of phrases and ideas already used in this chapter and in other places; the idea of the people as witnesses against themselves is at variance with v. 27 where the stone is witness; finally, the terminology used in this section suggests a late date.[78]

In the next section, vv. 25–27, the actual covenant making ceremony is completely contained. Not only because these verses do form a complete unit in this respect, but also because there is some tension between them and the rest of the chapter,[79] they should be treated as an independent unit. Certainly, there is some late terminology in the section, such as 'book of the law of God', but this can quite easily be separated from an older layer.[80] Within this section we find mainly the making of the covenant and the stone as witness to it. The only thing to which the stone could be witness is the proclaimed law of God which the people acknowledged, and so, even if 'statutes and ordinances' in v. 25 and 'book of the law of God' in v. 26 are to be taken as additions,[81] the declaration of divine law ('the words of Yahweh', v. 27) is presupposed here.[82]

In view of this, it may be concluded that Josh. 24, though heavily edited by the deuteronomist, preserves ancient elements: the putting away of foreign gods, the making of the covenant, the declaration of divine law, and the stone as witness to the covenant. These were the constituents of the covenant ceremony practised in old time at Shechem. It cannot of course be proved that the chapter is historically accurate in the position which it assigns Joshua in this ceremony. However, on the other hand, there is nothing to show that it was simply in order to legitimate a Shechemite cultic ceremony that Joshua was made to occupy the place he now has in Josh. 24.[83] The sanctuary itself was situated outside the city of Shechem, and the peaceful co-existence of the Israelites and the probably autonomous Shechem, at least until the time of Abimelech,[84] would have facilitated the establishment and the practice of the worship of Yahweh in the neighbourhood of the city.

It can, therefore, be accepted that at Shechem the covenant festival was celebrated.[85] This fulfils one of the conditions necessary for Shechem to be considered as the central sanctuary of an Israelite amphictyony. When it comes to the other two conditions, however, there is much less certainty. It is impossible to determine precisely what group or groups were involved in this covenant ceremony. The group which Joshua is supposed to be addressing

here is quite undefined. Joshua 24.1, it is true, refers in no uncertain manner to all Israel, but when it is remembered, first, that
Judg. 20.1f. similarly speaks of 'all the people of Israel' and 'the
chiefs of all the people, of all the tribes of Israel' who gathered at
Mizpah in order to decide how to deal with the tribe of Benjamin
which was clearly neither present nor represented at this
assembly,[86] and, secondly, that Josh. 24.1 may have been copied
from Josh. 23.2 anyway, it is clear that one cannot rely too heavily
on the accuracy of the statement in Josh. 24.1. In similar circumstances the only alternative would be to see which groups are
mentioned specifically in the course of the narrative, but since
Joshua and his house is the only specified group in this particular
instance, there is no way of giving a definite answer to the question
of who was involved in the covenant ceremony at Shechem. It may
be noted that Shechem lay in the territory of Machir (or Manasseh),[87] so Machir (or Manasseh) at least was involved with
Ephraim, the tribe of Joshua, in this ceremony, though nothing
more than this can be said.[88]

With the question of the presence of the ark at Shechem again
only a rather unsatisfactory answer can be given: there is no clear
indication that the ark was ever present there. Joshua 24.1 speaks
of Israel as having presented itself at Shechem 'before God', and
thus uses a phrase which in some of the psalms may have the
significance 'before the ark'.[89] However, this is certainly not a
necessary interpretation of the phrase in Josh. 24.1. Apart from
this the only other passage to which appeal can be made to show
the presence of the ark at Shechem is Josh. 8.30–35 which describes how, in fulfilment of the command of Moses, Joshua erected
an altar on Mount Ebal with stones on which were written the law
of Moses, while all Israel stood on either side of the ark. However,
this passage cannot be used with any confidence. It is manifestly
secondary in its present connection since it interrupts the story of
the conquest which suddenly breaks off in 8.29 and takes up again
in 9.1ff. As well as this, however, the whole passage must be
judged a late composition by the deuteronomist. It belongs to the
same literary stream in Deut. 27.1ff., which is likewise a late
section having no original connection with the old series of curses
which that chapter contains. While it is possible that in speaking of
an altar outside Jerusalem these late passages may preserve fragments of a pre-deuteronomistic tradition,[90] they must nevertheless

be judged as deuteronomistic in their present form.[91] Furthermore, since the deuteronomistic Deut. 27.1ff., in which is recorded Moses' command concerning the building of an altar on Mount Ebal after the entry into the land, contains no reference to the ark, the appearance of the ark in Josh. 8.30–35 should probably be understood as a still later addition to this section (perhaps from a second deuteronomistic editing) which has been brought in under the influence of the preceding chapters where the ark does play a significant role.[92] As for the reason for Josh. 8.30–35 being found in this particular place, it is likely that the deuteronomist wished to record the fulfilment of Moses' command by Joshua as soon as possible, and that it was considered by the deuteronomist that the way to Shechem was opened up to Israel through the conquest of Ai which he found described in the earlier part of Josh. 8. At any rate, our treatment of Josh. 8.30–35 means that there is no evidence that the ark was ever deposited at Shechem. Perhaps, however, one can go a stage further and say that in fact the ark was never found at Shechem, for if it had been there it would be difficult to explain why its presence there is not mentioned in Josh. 24.

For the sanctuary at Shechem, then, it may be concluded that the covenant festival was celebrated there, but that there is no evidence either that that sanctuary was acknowledged and visited by all the tribes of an Israelite amphictyony or their representatives, or that the ark was ever lodged there. As far as the ark is concerned, it may further be concluded that the probability is that it was never in fact to be found at Shechem. For the theory that the sanctuary at Shechem was the central sanctuary of an Israelite amphictyony, the only possible conclusion to be drawn is that if it can be proved by other means that an Israelite amphictyony existed in the period of the judges then it would be possible to claim that Shechem was one of its central sanctuaries. On the other hand, however, the traditions associated with Shechem do not on their own account suggest that Shechem was such a central sanctuary, and therefore it is impossible to use the hypothesis that Shechem was a central sanctuary in order to support the theory of the existence of an amphictyony.

The next place which must be considered as the possible site of a central sanctuary is Bethel. The central sanctuary is supposed[93] to have been transferred from Shechem to Bethel for one of two reasons: either the peaceful relations which had existed between

Israelites and the city of Shechem until then had broken down, or it was simply because the ark, the chief cult object of the central sanctuary, was in its original nature a travelling shrine which could not be lodged permanently at one place.

Bethel appears in a way in which it is possible to see it as a central sanctuary only in Judg. 20.18, 26f.; 21.2. All these passages belong to the narrative dealing with the revenge taken by Israel on the tribe of Benjamin and its city Gibeah for a crime committed against a Levite by the inhabitants of Gibeah. On this more will be said later. For the moment the point at issue concerns the place of Bethel in this story. According to Judg. 20.1 it was at Mizpah that the tribes gathered to discuss what should be done to Gibeah, while it is Bethel which is given as the sanctuary where the tribes went to seek an oracle of God and where they returned to lament and seek a fresh oracle from Yahweh ('for the ark of the covenant of God was there in those days'), after having been defeated by the men of Benjamin in battle. Finally, after Benjamin had been punished, it was at Bethel that the tribes lamented once more when they returned there to discuss how the breach in the ranks of the tribes of Israel created through the decimation of Benjamin should be repaired.

Before any judgment can be made on the place of Bethel in this story, the structure of Judg. 19–21 must be examined. Together with Judg. 17–18, these chapters were not originally part of the deuteronomistic historical work.[94] Naturally, however, the fact that they were brought into their present position later does not mean that they are devoid of any historical foundation, nor does it automatically mean that the story was composed at a late time. The only conclusion to be drawn from this is that Judg. 19–21 constitute a separate tradition which has been handed down independently of those traditions which are included within the deuteronomistic historical work. However, even within Judg. 19–21 different traditions are to be discerned, which have not successfully been harmonized in the present form of the text. Thus, for example, Judg. 21 presents two originally quite independent narratives, both of which deal with the same theme of how wives were supplied for those Benjaminites who survived the battle with the rest of Israel. According to the one version, in vv. 15ff., the 'daughters of Shiloh' were taken for the Benjaminites, while the other version, in vv. 1ff., describes how the unmarried women

of Jabesh-gilead were carried off for Benjamin. These two traditions are then rather inadequately brought together by the connecting link in Judg. 21.14b.

However, even with this view of things, there still remain
problems in the text of Judg. 21, especially in that section dealing
with Jabesh-gilead. It is quite clear that there is a double motif
within Judg. 21.1–14a.[95] On the one hand, vv. 1, 6–8, 12–13
describe how Jabesh-gilead was the one place not bound by the
oath taken by the rest of Israel at Mizpah that they would not give
their daughters in marriage to Benjamin. Thus, Jabesh-gilead was
able to supply wives for the Benjaminites. On the other hand, vv.
5, 9–11, 14a describe how Israel had taken an oath at Mizpah to
put to death those who did not take part in the assembly at
Mizpah where the decision was made on what should be done to
Benjamin and Gibeah. It was found that Jabesh-gilead had been
absent from this assembly, so a force was sent against that city to
destroy it and its inhabitants. However, the unmarried women of
Jabesh-gilead were saved alive to be wives for the survivors of
Benjamin. Clearly these are two quite independent traditions.
However, there still remains a part of vv. 1–14a which belongs to
neither of these traditions. This is to be found in vv. 2–4.[96] It is
true that since these verses do refer to the cutting off of one tribe
from Israel they cannot be judged as being totally independent of
their context, but they do not take account of survivors of Benjamin being supplied with wives, nor is their main point the battle
and its results described in the preceding chapter and in ch. 21. The
culminating point of Judg. 21.2–4 is the information that an altar,
on which were offered burnt offerings and peace offerings, was
erected at Bethel. So, four elements have contributed to the
present form of Judg. 21. There are three separate traditions dealing with how the survivors of Benjamin got wives, and then there
is the section 21.2–4.

To deal with ch. 21 apart from vv. 2–4: these three traditions
presuppose the complete destruction of the tribe of Benjamin
except for a very few survivors. However, this is certainly not the
essential theme of the preceding narrative. The latter is concerned
with the destruction of the town of Gibeah and the routing of the
army of Benjamin. The only place in which the complete destruction presupposed by ch. 21 is alluded to is in Judg. 20.48. This
verse, however, is a very generalized summary of the results of the

battle, and must be taken as an addition providing the foundation
for the traditions which follow in ch. 21. These latter must, therefore, be taken as an addition to the original story of chs. 19–20. All
three of them have an aetiological character: the one in vv. 15ff.
has the aim of explaining an otherwise unknown cultic custom at
Shiloh, while the other two are clearly concerned to explain the
particular connection which existed between the tribe of Benjamin
and the city of Jabesh-gilead, a connection which comes to the
fore in the history of the time of Saul.[97] So these traditions of ch.
21 must be seen as independent of chs. 19–20 the criticism of
which is a problem for itself.

Judges 19 raises no great difficulties. Apart from a few minor
glosses, it contains a uniform narrative. With ch. 20, however,
there is reason for more serious criticism. The story has been
supplemented with material which closely resembles other passages in the Old Testament, and which in fact has probably been
borrowed directly from these other passages.[98] However, as in
ch. 19, so in ch. 20 it is a case of a basic text having been supplemented; there is no basis for a division of the chapter into two
separate sources or versions.[99] The most important of these additions, from our point of view, is in Judg. 20.18. According to this
verse, Judah was commanded to go up first against Benjamin. But
Judah does not appear in such a capacity anywhere else in the
story, and that an oracle should be sought to find out which tribe
should go up first does not at all suit the context. Clearly, v. 18 is
an addition which is based on Judg. 1.1f. However, Judg. 20.18
also contains the first reference to Bethel in this narrative, and so
the words 'and came to Bethel' in Judg. 20.26 must also be treated
as an addition from the same hand as the one responsible for v. 18.
This is supported by the fact that Judg. 20.23, which is parallel
to v. 26, contains no reference to Bethel.[100] So the conclusion must
be that Bethel is not original in this narrative in ch. 20. The editor
responsible for the addition of Bethel here would also have been
responsible for the addition of vv. 2–4 in ch. 21, and since the
latter section presupposes the complete destruction of Benjamin,
the additions must have been made at some time after the aetiological stories in ch. 21 had been appended to the narrative of
Judg. 19–20. It is, moreover, possible to say something on the
question of who was responsible for these additions. The sections
dealing with Bethel culminate in Judg. 21.4. The editor has the aim

of showing Bethel as a sanctuary of the period of the judges where an altar was erected and where sacrifices were offered. He thus wishes to portray Bethel as an ancient and venerable site of Israelite worship of Yahweh. Bearing in mind that to show Bethel in this light is the exclusive purpose of these additions, there is apparently only one period which would provide a suitable context for the additions. This is the time of Jeroboam I. After the death of Solomon, when the empire established by David collapsed, Jeroboam, in order to further his aim of setting up a completely independent northern kingdom, established two royal sanctuaries which he intended should serve as a counter-attraction to pilgrims who would otherwise have gone up to Jerusalem. One of these royal sanctuaries was Bethel. But Jeroboam's royal sanctuaries, in order to gain the allegiance of the people, could not be completely new foundations. They would have to be recognized as ancient sites standing within Israel's cultic tradition. It was in order to demonstrate that this was the case that these additions were made in the time of Jeroboam I.[101]

That this is an accurate evaluation of the references to Bethel in Judg. 19–21 is perhaps confirmed by a consideration of Judg. 17–18. That these two chapters should not be treated in isolation is shown not only by the fact that they stand with chs. 19–21 outside the deuteronomistic historical work,[102] but also by the fact that they share a common theme with chs. 19–21: a Levite connected with both Bethlehem and Ephraim,[103] and a common formula: 'in those days there was no king in Israel; every man did what was right in his own eyes'.[104] In its use of this formula Judg. 17–18 reveals a very positive estimate of the monarchy; and, since the tradition is a specifically northern one dealing with the sanctuary of Dan, the monarchy in view is presumably that of the northern kingdom.[105] However, Dan was also one of the two royal sanctuaries established by Jeroboam I. The description, therefore, in Judg. 17–18 of how the sanctuary at Dan was established – a sudden attack by Danites on 'a people quiet and unsuspecting' which had no hope of deliverance, the setting up of a sanctuary equipped with a Levite who had been stolen from an Ephraimite, and an image of questionable legitimacy – should be seen as an attempt to denigrate the old foundation and so to justify and set in a favourable light the innovations carried out by Jeroboam when he turned the sanctuary of Dan into a royal sanctuary. Thus,

there is a clear parallel between the treatment of Dan in Judg.
17–18 and the treatment of Bethel in Judg. 19–21. Both aim at
justifying the setting up of these places as royal sanctuaries in the
time of Jeroboam I,[106] although different methods are used in
order to carry through this aim. This has the result that the story of
Judg. 19–21 cannot be used to determine the position of Bethel in
the period of the judges. It may indeed have been a sanctuary at
that time, but that is to be neither concluded nor excluded by
Judg. 19–21 where these chapters refer directly to Bethel.

However, there is still a part of Judg. 20 which has not been
considered yet, but which is very relevant to the point at issue
here. This is Judg. 20. 27b, 28a which, following on the present
form of v. 26, locate the ark at Bethel. We have already seen that
'and came to Bethel' in v. 26 is an addition based on v. 18, which
means that the original form of v. 26, like v. 23, referred to Mizpah,
the only alternative gathering place given for the Israelites in this
narrative.[107] But it does not follow that vv. 27b, 28a originally
located the ark at Mizpah, for these two half-verses are themselves
an addition breaking a connection in the text,[108] an addition which
was introduced probably by the editor responsible for the references to Bethel or by someone else at a later stage. Thus, Judg.
20.27b, 28a probably at all times intended to locate the ark at
Bethel. But since, on the other hand, the imparting of this information would not have been necessary in order to show Bethel
as the site of an ancient sanctuary, which was the purpose of the
editor, it must be concluded that in all probability Judg. 20.27b,
28a rest on an old tradition that the ark was in fact at one time
lodged at Bethel.[109]

In this respect, then, Bethel fulfils one of the conditions necessary for it to be treated as a central sanctuary. However, on the
other hand, there is no tradition which shows Bethel as a sanctuary acknowledged by all the tribes of Israel. The only text on the
basis of which it would have been possible to claim this is in Judg.
19–21, but this tradition clearly cannot withstand examination
from this point of view if the treatment given above is in any way
accurate. Moreover, there is nothing to indicate that Bethel was a
sanctuary where the covenant festival was celebrated. The basis
of the argument that Bethel succeeded Shechem as central sanctuary is that Gen. 35. 1–5 not only reflects a pilgrimage from
Shechem to Bethel, but also derives from a time when Bethel had

superseded Shechem in significance for Israel.[110] The coincidence
of the theme of the putting away of the foreign gods in Gen. 35.2
and Josh. 24.23 was taken to reveal that after Shechem was replaced by Bethel as central sanctuary, the major part of the cultic
rites and ceremonies associated with Shechem was also transferred to Bethel, though the former glory of Shechem was remembered through the retention at that sanctuary of a small portion of
its covenant ceremonial, and through the use of that sanctuary as
the starting point of a pilgrimage to Bethel. Clearly, however, this
interpretation cannot be accepted on the basis of Gen. 35.1–5 alone.
Certainly, these verses may reveal the practice of a pilgrimage from
Shechem to Bethel, but in order to justify the assertion that they
also reflect the transfer to Bethel of cultic ceremonies previously
associated with Shechem it must be shown from other texts that
those ceremonies, in this case the covenant festival, observed at
Shechem later found a home at Bethel. This cannot be established.

The state of confusion which really exists on this question of the
central sanctuary is perhaps well illustrated by the fact that arguments are also put forward for Shechem having been replaced as
central sanctuary by Gilgal,[111] which in turn was superseded by
Bethel.[112] The passages which are supposed to reflect these
transfers provide a foundation no stronger than does Gen. 35.1–5
for the view that Bethel followed immediately on Shechem. However, since Gilgal is widely understood to have been an amphictyonic central sanctuary, whatever position it may have occupied
in the succession of these sanctuaries, it is necessary to consider
here those texts which are drawn in as support. There are a number of these texts, to be found mainly in Josh. 2–9; outside this
group reference is also sometimes made to Judg. 2.1–5 and I Sam.
12.

For the celebration of the covenant festival at Gilgal, the texts
to which appeal is made are to be found in Josh. 5; Judg. 2.1–5
and I Sam. 12. This means that these passages must show that a
form of worship was practised at Gilgal similar to that practised
at Shechem as revealed by Josh. 24. That is, it must be shown that a
ceremony took place in Gilgal in which the people were bound to
the declared will of Yahweh. Seen from this point of view, however, Josh. 5 is of no help as evidence of the celebration of the
covenant festival at Gilgal; vv. 1–9, if they are not to be taken as
aetiological,[113] deal with circumcision; vv. 10–12, which are

probably late anyway,[114] are concerned with the celebration of the
Passover; while vv. 13–15 are best taken as a foundation saga or
legend explaining the use of that particular site for the worship of
Yahweh.[115] On the other hand, Judg. 2.1–5 does apparently offer
more hope for tracing the celebration of the covenant festival at
Gilgal. These verses relate how 'the angel of the Lord went up
from Gilgal to Bochim', where he brought accusation against
Israel for neglect of the covenant demands. Here, concise reference is made to Yahweh's saving deeds, as in Josh. 24.2ff., while
there is also a parallel between this passage and the covenant text
in Ex. 23.20ff. Thus, it is possible to understand this passage[116] as
an accusation against Israel for disregarding the implications of
the covenant festival which had been celebrated at Gilgal. However, it is doubtful if this interpretation can really stand. Quite
apart from the fact that no great weight can be laid on the parallel
with Josh. 24.2ff., which we have seen to be late, and also apart
from literary-critical considerations which would suggest that the
original passage consisted only of vv. 1a, 5b,[117] it is clear that the
rest of the passage, whether original or not, is an aetiological story
giving an Israelite-Yahwistic interpretation of the name Bochim.[118]
Probably this has replaced an earlier interpretation of the name,
but at any rate no conclusions on the form of worship practised
at Gilgal can be drawn from this passage with any confidence. This
leaves I Sam. 12 as the only remaining passage which may show
Gilgal as a place of covenant celebration.[119] However, this is clearly
a deuteronomistic composition set as a speech in the mouth of
Samuel.[120] The fact that the speech uses covenant language is
certainly no argument against its deuteronomistic character;[121]
so this passage cannot be used to show the celebration of the
covenant festival at Gilgal in the period of the judges.

One other argument in this connection must be mentioned:[122]
it has been proposed that since the 'cultic creed' of the form of
Deut. 26.5–9 had its *Sitz im Leben* at a sanctuary where the question of ownership of the land was a live issue, and so probably
belonged in the context of the Feast of Weeks celebrated at Gilgal,
and since this creed in fact forms the historical prologue, recount-
ing the saving acts of Yahweh, of the covenant form, therefore
the covenant was celebrated at Gilgal. However, this argument
may be attacked on a number of points. In the first place, does one
discern in the 'creed' an attempt to give theological justification

to the Israelite settlement of the land; in other words, is the question of the ownership of the land a 'live issue' or of 'pressing concern' in the creed?[123] This certainly does not come out from the contexts from which the creed has been taken. In Deut. 6.20ff., the recital of the saving acts of Yahweh serves simply as motivation for obedience to the commands of Yahweh. This is also the case in Josh. 24.2ff., while in Deut. 26.5–9 the concern is only to give the reason for offering the first fruits of the land to Yahweh. Secondly, even if the question of ownership of the land is a live issue in the creed, does this mean that the creed belongs to the sanctuary at Gilgal even though this was probably the home of the conquest narratives in Josh. 2–9?[124] This is hardly the case unless one is prepared to argue, for example, that the tradition of God's promise of the land to Abraham and his descendants, in which the question of the ownership of the land is just as much an issue as in the creed,[125] also belonged to Gilgal. The point is that ownership of the land could have been an issue at any sanctuary, not only at Gilgal. Thirdly, granted that the creed does belong to Gilgal, does this show that the covenant festival belonged there also? Again, this conclusion cannot be accepted. The fact that the creed is used in Deut. 26.5–9 to give the reason for the offering of the first fruits, and the fact that Josh. 24.2–13 and 16f. share a common form, but of which only the latter can really be called a creed, would indicate that what has been called a creed is in fact a literary form which could be used on different occasions and for different purposes.[126] Finally, and most important, it is becoming more and more doubtful that one can claim Deut. 26.5–9 as an early creed which forms the basis of the Pentateuch.[127] Not only is this passage 'stuck away in a rather odd corner'[128] to be so basic and important, but its language and expression find their closest parallels in deuteronomistic literature,[129] which would mean that it is most likely a comparatively late composition.

Altogether, then, this so-called creed says little or nothing about forms of worship practised in Gilgal before the rise of the monarchy, and the other evidence which has been brought forward is clearly not enough to justify the claim that Yahweh was worshipped at Gilgal in the form of a covenant festival.

On the other hand, an affirmative answer should probably be given to the question of whether the ark was ever present at Gilgal. It is true that a literary-critical and traditio-historical

analysis of Josh. 3–4 can justifiably reduce this narrative to a number of aetiological fragments in which the ark has little or no place,
and which have been supplemented in the course of several redac-
tions.[130] However, since the ark does now occupy a prominent
place in these chapters, and since its introduction would not
have been essential to the development of the originally independent aetiological stories basic to the narrative,[131] it must be
considered most likely that the references to the ark in the present
form of the narrative presuppose that at one time the ark was
actually to be found at Gilgal.[132]

That Gilgal was a sanctuary acknowledged and visited by the
members of an Israelite amphictyony is, however, much less
certain. According to I Sam. 11.14ff., it was at Gilgal that Saul was
made king. This does not, however, necessarily imply that Gilgal
was an amphictyonic sanctuary.[133] Most of the rest of the land was
in Philistine control at the time, and, furthermore, Saul belonged
to the tribe of Benjamin in the territory of which Gilgal lay.[134]
Gilgal was one of the probably very few places where such an
action could have been carried out in defiance of the Philistines.
So I Sam. 11 does not reveal anything of the status of the sanctuary
at Gilgal before the rise of Saul.

For the place of Gilgal among the other sanctuaries reference
must be made once again to Josh. 3–4. In this narrative twelve men
were chosen by Joshua, one from each of the Israelite tribes, who
would take twelve stones from the middle of the Jordan and set
them up in the 'place where they lodged' as a memorial of the
miraculous crossing of the Jordan into the land. It is only this
association of twelve stones, which, in one tradition, were set up
in Gilgal (Josh. 4.8), and, in another tradition, were set up in the
midst of the Jordan (Josh. 4.9), with the twelve tribes of Israel,
which can support the view that Gilgal was a central sanctuary of
an Israelite amphictyony of twelve tribes in the period of the
judges.

It is not necessary to deal in detail with the literary-critical
difficulties of Josh. 3–4.[135] Our concern is simply with those elements of the narrative which deal with the selection of twelve men
and twelve stones, and our aim is to determine the character of
these elements and their relationship to the narrative as a whole.
It is true that if Josh. 3–4 is to be seen as the description of a
regularly repeated cultic act in which the ark was carried through

the Jordan in order to 'actualize' or 're-present' the crossing of the Reed Sea and the entry into the land,[136] then it would be difficult to isolate fragments of these chapters and treat them independently. However, quite apart from the practical difficulties which would attend the performance of such a cultic act, this view takes no account of either the literary-critical questions posed by the text, or the very nature of the traditions which form the present narrative.[137]

Those parts of the narrative which are our concern here may, in fact, be isolated quite easily. They deal with the choosing of twelve men and the setting up of twelve stones, and are to be found only in Josh. 4. The story of the actual crossing of the Jordan is completed in Josh. 3;[138] so the original independence of this tradition from those dealing with the choice of men and the erection of stones is quite recognizable even in the present form of the narrative. These have been brought into a loose connection through the late insertion in ch. 3 of v. 12, a verse which has no affinity either with what precedes or with what follows in that chapter, but which was inserted simply in order to gloss over the secondary connection made between the tradition of the crossing of the Jordan and the other traditions to be found in ch. 4. This does not mean that the stories of Joshua's choosing twelve men and of the erection of twelve stones ever existed as independent traditions; it is simply that these stories formed no original part of the tradition of the crossing of the Jordan. This view is confirmed by a consideration of the form of the traditions which Josh. 4 contains. There are, basically, two aetiological tales which have the aim of explaining and accounting for the existence of twelve prominent stones set up at Gilgal and a similar group of stones set up in the river Jordan.[139] The primary element of these stories is the existence of twelve stones at Gilgal, whose significance probably originally had to do with astral phenomena,[140] and the existence of a group of stones also in the Jordan. The secondary element, on the other hand, is that which attempts to explain how and why these stones came to be set up at these particular places. Two conditions had to be fulfilled before this secondary element, the explanation of the stones, could exist and be brought into connection with the tradition of the crossing of the Jordan. On the one hand, the conquest traditions of Josh. 2–9, which probably had their focal point at Gilgal, had to be recognized and accepted as the conquest tradition of all Israel; and, on the other hand, the view that Israel was a people of twelve tribes must have been an established one. However, it is precisely this latter point which shows that that part of Josh. 3–4 which deals with the twelve men and the twelve stones cannot be used in order to demonstrate that Gilgal in the period of the judges was a central sanctuary of an amphictyony of Israelite tribes. Gilgal was certainly a sanctuary in the period of the judges, but its association in Josh. 4 with the twelve tribes of Israel is a secondary one which presupposes only that at some time or other, and not necessarily in the period of the judges, Israel was considered to consist of twelve tribes. This we already know from other sources such as the lists of twelve tribes.

The overall conclusion, therefore, which must be drawn as far as Gilgal is concerned is that if it can be shown from other sources that an Israelite amphictyony existed in the period of the judges, then it would be possible to accommodate the sanctuary at Gilgal as one of its central sanctuaries. On the other hand, however, there is nothing in what we know of Gilgal in this time which compels the assumption that such an amphictyony did exist with Gilgal as the central sanctuary.

The only other place which may be considered in this connection is Shiloh.[141] We have already seen the importance which has been ascribed to it by many scholars.[142] Towards the end of the period of the judges the ark was to be found in a temple there (I Sam. 3.3), and from there it was taken to battle against the Philistines, as a result of which it was captured.[143] However, while the presence of the ark at Shiloh can hardly be disputed,[144] there is much less clarity about the possibility of claiming Shiloh as a sanctuary visited by all the Israelite tribes, and as a sanctuary where the covenant festival was celebrated.

I Samuel 1–4 represents the only Old Testament passage which may reliably be used to determine the position of Shiloh in the early period. Texts at the end of Joshua, such as Josh. 18.1, are late,[145] while Judg. 21.16ff. aims simply at giving the aetiology of a cultic custom at Shiloh[146] and has no bearing either on the celebration there of the covenant festival or on the use of that sanctuary by all Israel.[147] However, I Sam. 1–4 also provides little help. In I Sam. 1.3 Elkanah is said to 'go up year by year from his city to worship and to sacrifice to the Lord of hosts at Shiloh'; but, even if this was not a family festival,[148] there is no foundation for seeing it as a festival of a national character, nor for treating it as a covenant festival in particular. I Samuel 4 describes how the ark was brought from Shiloh to the battle with the Philistines, but Shiloh is not the place where Israel assembled for this battle, quite apart from the question of what tribes actually did participate in the battle.

Clearly, then, our conclusion for the sanctuary at Shiloh must be the same as that for the sanctuary at Gilgal: if it can be shown by other means that an amphictyony existed in Israel of the period of the judges, then it is possible to consider Shiloh as a central sanctuary. But nothing in the texts dealing with Shiloh suggests that it was a central sanctuary, and so these texts cannot be used in order to support the theory of the Israelite amphictyony.

By using the criteria which have been adopted here the only possible conclusion is that there is no compelling evidence that any of the sanctuaries suggested occupied the position of central sanctuary in an Israelite amphictyony. Even if the criteria of the celebration of the festival of covenant renewal and of the presence of the ark are not to be used to determine if a sanctuary was a central sanctuary,[149] this conclusion is still valid; for of none of the sanctuaries which have been proposed can it be shown that it was a sanctuary maintained and visited by all Israel. The latter must be the chief point, and evidence that a sanctuary was acknowledged as central sanctuary would take the form of some positive indication (1) that a sanctuary was the meeting place of tribal representatives; (2) that it was maintained by the tribes; and (3) that it was visited regularly by these tribes on festival occasions. However, there is no unambiguous evidence that any of the sanctuaries proposed occupied such a position. There is no indication that any of them was the meeting place for tribal representatives. It is also clear that while some group must have been responsible for the maintenance of each of the sanctuaries it is impossible from the records at our disposal to conclude that any of them was maintained by a number of tribes rather than by the particular tribe in whose territory the sanctuary lay. As for the third point, it is, of course, true that some sanctuaries may have been visited by pilgrims from outside the district in which they were to be found; but there is no sign that any sanctuary was a focal point for regular visits by members of a federation which was responsible for the maintenance of that sanctuary. Instead, it is most likely that all these sanctuaries enjoyed much the same significance and popularity in their own districts, and while, for example, the presence of the ark may have constituted a temporary attraction for pilgrims to a particular sanctuary,[150] this does not necessarily involve the idea that that sanctuary was considered in any way as a central sanctuary in the manner of the amphictyonic shrines at Delphi and Pylae.

If this is the case, then it also makes somewhat questionable the interpretation of *nāśi'* as representative of the tribe at the central sanctuary.[151] Noth's view of the meaning of the word is based mainly on its use in late passages, but he argues that it is unlikely that it was only at this comparatively late time that a special technical significance was attached to the word. According to Noth, the word derives from the customary language of the old Israelite amphictyony, and it should not be surprising that, apart from the few passages in the Old Testament which stem directly from the tradition of the amphictyony, the word should first appear again in P; the older historical, prophetic and poetic literature had no occasion to use it.[152]

It is clear, of course, that this argument presupposes, but cannot be held to prove or even to support the existence of an Israelite amphictyony. But besides this, it is to be noted that it is only in passages of late date that the word can easily bear the significance of tribal representative in Noth's sense. Where the word occurs in what is clearly a relatively early source there is not the slightest indication that it had the meaning which Noth ascribes to it. One can quickly point to a passage, such as Gen. 34.2, where *nāśi'* apparently has the general meaning of leader or prince. However, the most important occurrence in this connection is perhaps Ex. 22.27 (EVV v. 28): 'you shall not curse God nor revile a *nāśi'* of your people'. This verse belongs to the book of the covenant, a collection of law[153] which originated, if in fact it was not substantially completed, before the rise of the monarchy.[154] Noth himself would have it that the book of the covenant is best understood as having originated within the framework of the amphictyony, and that those religious and moral prohibitions which are expressed in the form of Ex. 22.27 (EVV v. 28) derive from the ancient Israelite amphictyonic law.[155] This means that *nāśi'* with the meaning of tribal representative should be apparent in Ex. 22.27 if anywhere. While the indefinite formulation of this

verse does not altogether prohibit the understanding which has
been suggested by Noth, it certainly does not support it; for if
Noth's suggestion were correct the most natural formulation of
Ex. 22.27 would be: 'you shall not curse God nor revile the
neśî'îm (plural) of your people'. In its present form Ex. 22.27 presents the *nāśî'* as a chief or leader in general, but no representative
function is indicated except in so far as every leader is a representative. Apart from the late P passages there is nothing to indicate
that the *nāśî'* was the representative of an individual tribe.[156] This
understanding is not contradicted by the general content of the
book of the covenant, for this compilation does not necessarily
presuppose the existence of an amphictyony as such; the
group whose activities are regulated by it could be large or
small.[157]

c. *The Judge of Israel*

Hitherto nothing definite has been found to suggest that early
Israel was organized along the lines of the Greek amphictyonies.
While it is still possible that the list of tribes in Num. 1.5–15 presents a selection of tribes reckoned as Israelite in the latter half of
the period of the judges, there is not yet any evidence of the existence of an office or an institution based on a unity of these tribes
and giving practical expression to this unity. However, besides
the conjectured institution of the central sanctuary and office of
nāśî', which, as we have seen, cannot stand up to examination,
there is still another office proposed for this period which must be
considered. If this office existed it would certainly constitute a
bond between the tribes and thus provide general support for the
amphictyony theory. The office in question is that of the *śōpēṭ
yiśrā'ēl*, the 'judge of Israel', 'Israel' being the amphictyonic
organization of the tribes.[158]

In Judg. 10.1–5; 12.7–15 there are named six men who are said
to have 'judged Israel'. Besides the name, the only information
given about each man concerns his home, the number of years
spent in office and his place of burial. With three of them some
other legendary details concerning numerous posterity have also
been attached.[159] It is clear that Judg. 10.1–5; 12.7–15 originally
formed a connected list.[160] Its present broken state resulted from
the fact that Jephthah the Gileadite was not only numbered among

these judges but was also the subject of a tradition portraying him as a deliverer in the manner of the other deliverers such as Gideon and Samson. This deliverer story was incorporated into the original list of judges at the point where Jephthah was named.[161] The incorporation of this tradition meant the suppression of the formula by which the judges were usually introduced: 'after him NN judged Israel', which in the original list would have come between Judg. 10.5 and 12.7. However, before the significance of this list can be determined there is a preliminary point to be discussed. Can the list of Judg. 10.1–5; 12.7–15 be taken as complete? The fact that one break has been made in it in order to incorporate a particular tradition about one of the members of the list opens the possibility that in the same way other figures are now separated from their rightful place within this list of judges. There is a problem, however, in finding a reliable method which will help us to decide which if any of the individuals not at present in the list should be included in it. This question can be approached in two ways: on the one hand, the functions of the members of the list may be compared with those of figures outside the list; and, on the other hand, we may examine the literary forms by which each member of the list is introduced and his life and activities described, and then see which figures outside the list are introduced and described with the same literary forms.

For the first approach, the significance of the root *špṭ* must be discussed. It is this verb which is used to describe the functions of the judges in the list, and which is also used to describe the functions of several other figures, particularly Othniel, Deborah, Samson and Samuel. If it can be shown that in both contexts the verb has the same significance, this would be a strong argument in favour of understanding these individuals as having originally belonged in the list of those who 'judged Israel'.

The question of the significance of the term *špṭ* as used in both of these contexts has aroused some controversy, and has by no means been finally settled. It has been widely understood that the term has basically a legal connotation, with the sense of 'act as a law-giver', 'pronounce judgment', and so it has been thought[162] that originally, and properly, it was applied to the activities of those men mentioned in the list of judges. At a later stage, however, because Jephthah was numbered among the judges of the list and also among those other deliveries of the Book of Judges, this term was carried over editorially to describe also the activities of those charismatic deliverers such as Samson, an application of the term which does not reflect historical reality. Whether or not this view is accepted, it nevertheless clearly points up the issue here: what is the meaning of the term when used in the context of the list of Judg. 10.1–5; 12.7–15? Has the term the same meaning in the context of the charismatic deliverers? If it has the same meaning, are the charismatic deliverers to be understood as original members of the list? If it has not, what is the meaning of the term when used outside the list?

It has, in fact, been argued that the root *špṭ* has the general meaning of 'rule' besides the specific meaning of 'judge'; and in order to justify this, appeal is made particularly to the Ugaritic texts, though it is also argued that this general meaning conforms well with the context of the use of the root in some Old Testament passages.[163] However, in spite of this, it still remains true that as far as the Old Testament itself is concerned there are only about three out of some two hundred occurrences of the root where the meaning 'rule' is perhaps preferable, but where it is certainly not essential.[164] In the majority of cases the root has the legal significance of 'pronounce judgment', 'give a decision'. Yet, while this is apparently its primary significance, there are a number of passages in the Old Testament where such a restricted meaning is not suitable. In Isa. 1.17, 23, for example,[165] 'judge the fatherless' can only mean 'help the fatherless to their rights', or 'defend, or deliver the fatherless from oppression'; and the idea of deliverance is also clearly required by II Sam. 18.19, 31. This is again the case in I Sam. 24.16 (EVV v. 15) where the root is used twice, once in the sense of 'decide between', and once in the sense of 'deliver'. Furthermore, it is to be noted that the occurrences in II Sam. 18 do not stand in a legal context, although this may be the context of Isa. 1.17, 23. It is, therefore, evident that the root *špṭ* does have the general sense of 'deliver' besides the specific legal sense of 'pronounce judgment'.

In the light of this, what can be said of the use of the root in connection with the list of Judg. 10.1–5; 12.7–15 on the one hand, and the charismatic deliverers on the other? First of all, it must be noted that the list and the stories of the deliverers are, from a literary point of view, quite distinct. The list is an independent literary unit which is in its present form broken by the insertion of a foreign literary element, the story of Jephthah. The latter belongs with the independent literary category formed by the stories of the deliverers. Therefore, the meaning of the root *špṭ* is not necessarily the same in both of these contexts, nor is its meaning in one context necessarily to be decided by reference to its use in the other context.

As far as the list of Judg. 10.1–5; 12.7–15 is concerned, the reason for the preservation of the names of the judges in the list, and the only reason for this preservation, is that they performed certain actions which are not described but which are referred to by means of this root *špṭ*. This is the case even with Jephthah, for in so far as he appears in the independent literary unit formed by the list it is because his activities coincided with those of the other members of the list, and not because of his exploits as a deliverer. Jephthah, as a deliverer, was assured of a place among the deliverers, not among the members of the list. In fact, it is precisely the appearance of Jephthah both in the list of those who 'judged' Israel and among the deliverers which would lead us to the conclusion that the activities of those men who are said to have judged Israel belonged in the legal sphere; they were judges, and it was as such that they were remembered in the tradition. Had they been deliverers there would have been traditions telling of their exploits as there are of Jephthah and the other deliverers.

As far as the charismatic deliverers are concerned, however, the case seems somewhat different. The names of these men are preserved because of their exploits related in the traditions associated with them.[166] This in itself is enough to suggest that the root *špṭ*, when used in summary fashion to describe their activities,[167] either is used legitimately with the sense of 'deliver' (which, as we have seen, is a sense that the root does apparently have on occasions), or has been applied to them with the sense of 'judge' for some reason unconnected with the nature of their activities. In other words, because the reason for the names of these men having been preserved is to be found in the records about them as charismatic deliverers, it is unlikely that the root *špṭ*, when used in connection with them, has the same connotation as it has when applied to the members of the list; or if it has the same connotation then the application of the root to the charismatic deliverers does not correspond with their historical activities, but should be seen rather as the work of the editor of these traditions.

The implication of this for our purposes here is that it is most unlikely that the charismatic deliverers whose activities are described by use of the term *špṭ* should be included within the list of judges simply on the basis of the meaning of *špṭ*. It may be argued that in spite of this a functional connection existed between the two groups in that the judge became judge on the basis of his manifestation of charisma in the manner of the deliverers; but for this there is no support in the actual text apart from the probably exceptional case of Jephthah.[168] That the latter case is exceptional is indicated by the fact that no traditions of charismatic activities similar to his have been preserved for the other judges of the list in Judg. 10.1–5; 12.7–15.

That these two groups, the judges and the charismatic deliverers, should be kept separate is also indicated by the fact that the literary forms which are used to introduce the judges of the list are not generally reproduced with the charismatic deliverers. This brings us to the second possible approach to this problem: a comparison between the literary forms used in connection with the members of the list and the literary forms used in connection with individuals outside the list.

There is a noticeable similarity in the way each member of the list of judges is presented, even though there are also some noteworthy variations.[169] Regular throughout the list is that each judge is connected with his predecessor by the words 'after him':[170] but apart from this, the introduction of each judge is not carried through in the same words. While Judg. 10.1, 3 use the word *wayyāqom* – 'and there arose' – Judg. 12.8, 11, 13 use the word *wayyišpōṭ* – 'and there judged'.[171] Following on this, details of descendants are provided for Jair in 10.4, for Ibzan in 12.9, and for Abdon in 12.14; but no information of this sort is provided for the other judges in the list. However, the notice that the judge 'judged Israel for . . . years' occurs with every occupant of the list, and the same is the case with the concluding notice of the death and place of burial of each judge. So the list then contains the following three constants: (1) each judge is connected with his predecessor by the words 'after him'; (2) of each judge it is said that 'he judged Israel for . . . years'; (3) of each judge it is recorded that '(he) died and was buried in . . .'. These, then, are the points which are especially important in a comparison of the literary forms used of the judges with those used of individuals outside the list of judges.

On the basis of such a comparison it has been proposed[172] that the list of judges originally comprised twelve members, including, besides those at present in the list, Joshua, Othniel, Ehud, Gideon, Samson and Samuel. When, however, the tradition on Joshua is examined,[173] it appears that there is nothing said on Joshua's having judged Israel for a number of years, while the third element of the scheme outlined above occurs, but in a changed form, in Josh. 24.29f. For Othniel, the second element in Judg. 3.10 does not include the years in office, while the third element in Judg. 3.11b is not found in its full form. For Ehud, the second element of the scheme is to be found only in a Septuagint addition at the end of Judg. 3.30, and that in an incomplete and changed form, while the third element in Judg. 4.1 is also quite different and incomplete. For Gideon, the third element is complete in Judg. 8.32, and in Judg. 8.30 there is a reference to his descendants in the manner sometimes found with the judges of the list; however, it is not said of Gideon that he judged Israel for a number of years. With Samson, the second element is complete in Judg. 15.20, but the third is incomplete and different in Judg. 16.31. Finally, for Samuel, the second element is complete in I Sam. 7.15, while the third is found in slightly changed form in I Sam. 25.1.

From this it is clear that, with the possible exception of Samuel, none of these men can be claimed as having been originally members of the list of judges, simply on the basis of the literary forms used to describe the life and activity of each one.[174] It is true that it could be claimed that changes in the literary forms used were bound to occur when these supposed members of the original list were separated from it, and that the fact that this method results in a list consisting of twelve members, analogous to the lists of twelve tribes, in itself supports the method. However, as far as the last part of this argument is concerned, it is clearly invalid. If Joshua, Othniel, Ehud, Gideon and Samson are to be included in the list, then so also should Deborah,[175] for with her also there is found, in Judg. 4.4, the second element of the scheme, although in a changed form. Furthermore, the second element of the scheme is used also with Eli in I Sam. 4.18. This would then give a list of fourteen members. As far as the first part of the argument is concerned, it is undoubtedly correct in its presupposition that the present Book of Judges is the result of an editorial conflation of two categories of traditional material.[176] On the one hand, there was a series of narratives dealing with tribal heroes and their victories over enemies, and on the other hand there was a list of judges, of which there is at least a part preserved in Judg. 10.1–5; 12.7–15. From a literary point of view these two complexes of tradition are quite different. But it is equally clear that in bringing these two complexes of tradition together, the editor was not bound to preserve their original independent nature, but felt free to conflate them. Even if none of those men proposed as judges are taken as having been originally members of the list, this freedom on the part of the editor can be recognized from the fact that he was able to insert in the middle of the list the particular tradition about Jephthah. Obviously, then, it was the aim of the editor to integrate both complexes of tradition into his own chronological scheme for the period of the judges. However, it is precisely this latter point which indicates that the various statements on Joshua, Othniel, Ehud, Gideon and Samson,[177] which are reminiscent of similar statements about the judges in the list, may be the result, not of these men having been removed from their original places in the list, but of a deliberate policy on the part of the editor who wished to gloss over as far as possible the obvious differences between the two complexes of tradition he was using as his sources for this period.[178] In other words, the statements may have been formed in analogy to the way in which the judges of the list as we now have it are introduced and described.

In the present state of our knowledge this, in fact, seems the safest conclusion. The use of the term *špṭ* to describe the activities of the charismatic deliverers is probably the work of an editor who wished to harmonize to some extent the two sources which he conflated in order to present a history of the period of the judges; on the other hand, the editor's use of the root *špṭ* was not totally illegitimate since this can have, as we have seen, the significance 'deliver'.[179]

Although those men who appear in the list in Judg. 10 and 12 are said to have 'judged Israel', they are nowhere called 'judges of Israel'. In spite of this, however, Noth has argued[180] that this is an authentic and ancient list containing the names of those men who in the period of the judges occupied in succession the amphictyonic office of 'judge of Israel'. This precise title is met with only once in the Old Testament, in Micah 4.14 (EVV 5.1). Here Noth thinks that it cannot refer to the Davidic king since if the prophet was thinking of the king he would have been unambiguous about it. Rather, the prophet here uses the title of those who judged Israel, of whom there are early representatives in Judg. 10 and 12. On the basis of Micah 4.14 and also Deut. 17.8–13, it may be concluded that the office of 'judge of Israel' must, like the amphictyony itself, have persisted right into the period of the monarchy. Neither the amphictyony nor its judge were supplanted by the monarchy and the king at the end of the period of the judges. Amphictyonic institutions continued to exist side by side with the monarchy;[181] and the fact that we have in the list of judges in Judg. 10 and 12 what can only be an authentic record of the number of years for which each judge held office suggests to Noth that the judge of Israel was the holder of an office of central importance in the amphictyony, and that probably also reference was made to the name and year of the office-bearer in the dating of events.[182]

If this view could be substantiated on its own merits, that is, if it could be shown that these judges occupied an office of significance for all Israel, apart from the prior acceptance of the theory of the amphictyony, then this would of itself provide very strong support for the theory in general. It is important, therefore, to determine in what sense the term 'Israel' is to be understood when it is said that these men 'judged Israel'. The first point to be discussed, however, is the evidence for the existence of an office the occupants of which bore the title 'judge of Israel'. This title is not used of those judges of the list in Judg. 10.1–5; 12.7–15, who are said only to have 'judged Israel'. The only occurrence of the title is in Micah 4.14 (EVV 5.1), and so our immediate question concerns the person to whom reference is made in this prophetic passage. Is Micah referring to the occupant of an amphictyonic office or is he in fact referring to the Davidic king? In favour of the former interpretation of the words, there is undoubtedly the fact that the present context of the verse does not mention the Davidic king, and unless the occupant of an independent office of 'judge of Israel' were meant here the reference might be somewhat ambiguous to the prophet's audience. However, this point depends on the context to which the verse is to be assigned and on the interpretation of this context.

It is unlikely that the verse is to be seen as the immediate continuation or conclusion of the preceding verses. These verses end with a summons to the 'daughter of Zion' to be victorious over her enemies, and 4.13 forms the most natural conclusion to the unit formed by 4.11–13. Apart from this, however, many different proposals have been made on 4.14; here we need mention briefly only two.[183] Beyerlin has argued[184] that 4.14 stands at present in a secondary context. It originally belonged at the end of the song of lament in Micah 1.8–16. There are six arguments to support this: (1) Micah 1.16 and 4.14 allude to different mourning customs[185] which are treated together in Lev. 19.27, 28; 21.5; Deut. 14.1; (2) the Qinah metre is used in both 1.8–16 and 4.14; (3) in both 1.8–16 and 4.14 there is word-play; (4) feminine forms are to be found in both 1.16 and 4.14; (5) 1.15b and 4.14 are both to be understood as referring to Jerusalem;[186] (6) the historical background of both 1.8–16 and 4.14 is the same, namely, the invasion of Sennacherib in 701 BC. The verse 4.14 was attracted to its present context from its original position, in the first place because it begins with the word *'attāh*, 'now', which occurs as the introduction to most of the verses in 4.8–5.1 and, secondly, in order that the defeated 'judge of Israel' should serve as a foil to the successful 'ruler in Israel' who is described in 5.1ff. (EVV vv. 2ff.).

However, while admitting the strength of these arguments, it is precisely the reasons given for the transfer of 4.14 from its alleged original place immediately after 1.8–16 to its present context which can be taken to support the conclusion reached by Willis[187] that 4.14 should not be separated from 5.1ff. If 4.14 is then taken along with what follows, it can be seen that these verses form a particular unit with a form which is to be found also in 3.9 (or 12)–4.5 and 4.11–13, that is 'a short section of doom followed by a long section of hope'; slightly different forms are to be found also in 4.6–8, 9–10; 5.6–8, 9–14. On the other hand, however, it could of course be argued that the present arrangement of these sections, with the alternation of doom and hope, is ultimately the work of the collector of the prophetic sayings who, for his own purposes, took 4.14 from its original place at the end of 1.8–16. If this is admitted as a possibility, then a certain decision on the original place of 4.14 is not possible.

For our own purposes, however, this uncertainty is not of great importance since our conclusion on the significance of the 'judge of Israel' in 4.14 is the same whether this verse is to be taken as the conclusion of 1.8–16 or as the beginning of 5.1ff. In both places, reference is undoubtedly made in this verse to the Davidic king.[188] In 1.8–16 Jerusalem and the 'kings of Israel' are mentioned, and the designation of the Davidic king as *šōpēṭ*, 'judge', can be seen as prompted not only by word-play but also by the fact that the king was very intimately involved in the dispensation of justice. If the verse is taken along with 5.1ff., then a contrast is drawn between the present judge of Israel under whom Israel is suffering at the hands of her enemies, and the future ruler in Israel who, under Yahweh, will bring security to Israel. Here also reference to the Davidic king is much more likely than reference to the occupant of an amphictyonic office of judge of Israel who would scarcely have been contrasted in such a way with the future ruler, and whose function would scarcely have been that of delivering Israel from her enemies. This latter point raises the possibility that *šōpēṭ* here is in fact not to be understood in the sense of 'judge', but, as with the charismatic deliverers in the Book of Judges, in the sense of 'deliverer'. Such a sense would suit well both here and in the context of Micah 1.8–16; he who is responsible for the deliverance of Israel is himself defeated. But even if the title is to be translated 'judge of Israel', its application to the Davidic king is entirely suitable. The actual title is not to be found outside Micah 4.14, but not only do several passages show the Davidic king as the one before whom cases were taken for decision and judgment,[189] but the ruler whom the people request from Samuel (I Sam. 8.20) is a king who 'will judge us',[190] while Solomon prayed for an 'understanding mind to judge thy people' (I Kings 3.9). In the list of David's officers which is given in II Sam. 8.15–18 nothing is said of the appointment of a judge of Israel, and it is most unlikely that in the period of the monarchy the appointment to such an office, if it existed, would lie anywhere but with the king. Instead, it is David himself who 'administered justice and equity to all his people' (II Sam. 8.15); and it seems that it was by taking advantage of his father's failure to fulfil this duty that Absalom tried to win support for himself from disappointed claimants (II Sam. 15.1ff.).[191] This does not necessarily mean that all judicial functions devolved on the king alone. He probably represented the court of appeal, or the one to whom particularly difficult cases were brought for judgment; no doubt the elders at the city gate still played a part in the local administration of justice.[192] There is no evidence, however, of the existence in the monarchy period of an amphictyonic office of 'judge of Israel'; if such an office existed at all, then it must have been occupied by the king himself.

For the earlier period the ground is less certain. The members of the list in Judg. 10.1–5; 12.7–15 are all said to have 'judged Israel', but can one immediately conclude from this that they occupied an office of significance for all Israel and bore the title 'judge of Israel'? This is the conclusion which is drawn by Noth, who has also argued[193] that the deuteronomist carried over to the charismatic deliverers the all-Israel significance which he found already present with the judges of the list. So a method must be found of checking the authenticity of the list in Judg. 10 and 12 when it speaks of these men having judged 'Israel'. It must be determined if the list is historically accurate when it gives the activities of the judges significance for all Israel.

The present form of the list of judges in Judg. 10.1–5; 12.7–15 is of no help at this point. The fact that the place of birth and burial of each judge is given does not necessarily mean that the activity of the judges was confined to these places.[194] That their sphere of activity was so confined may in fact be true, but this is not to be concluded from the list itself. On the other hand, a probable conclusion may be reached on the basis of what the tradition records on Samuel. The possibility has already been noted that of all the individuals outside the list of judges it is Samuel who has most claim to having originally been a member of this list. Not only do the literary forms used in the context of the Samuel tradition correspond to the forms used in the list of judges, but the further details which the tradition provides conform well with Samuel's representation as a judge.[195] Furthermore, it is precisely these details which give a credible picture of Samuel's sphere of influence and activity, and in this way define what is meant by the description of him as one who 'judged Israel'. I Samuel 7.16 records that Samuel used to go 'on a circuit year by year to Bethel, Gilgal and Mizpah; and he judged Israel in all these places'. That the references to these three places should be ascribed to the deuteronomist or some other editor is unlikely; in fact, the only reason for the preservation of this information is that Samuel's circuit taking in these places formed part of the old Samuel tradition.[196] If this is the case, then it is as justifiable to use this verse as a historical source as it is to use the list of judges in Judg. 10.1–5; 12.7–15. The places where Samuel exercised this function of judge all lay within the territory of the mid-Palestinian tribes; so his circuit was a strictly local one.[197] As well as this, however, the only reason for Samuel's having made this circuit year by year would have been that he could act as judge for the benefit of those living in the immediate vicinity of the places mentioned. The 'Israel' which Samuel judged was in reality the local population of the places included in his circuit.[198] Unless this were the case, Samuel's circuit would have been superfluous. Furthermore, if I Sam. 8.2 is to be seen as part of the same old Samuel tradition,[199] then Samuel's sons were contemporary judges acting in a southern area outside the province covered by Samuel himself.[200] Since we have already seen that Samuel should probably be considered as one of the judges of the list in Judg. 10 and 12, then the sphere of activity of the judges of this list should be determined in the light of what is known about Samuel. That is, these men, too, exercised their judicial functions within a limited area, in most cases probably within the territory occupied by their respective tribes.[201] These men 'judged Israel' in the same sense as did Samuel, and, this being the case, the possibility cannot be excluded that, although the present form of the tradition presents them as occupying a particular office in succession,[202] some of them may in fact have been contemporaries acting in different provinces.[203] On this point, however, the tradition gives us no sure guide.

As for the precise functions of these judges the tradition is equally obscure.[204] It is unlikely that military exploits formed part of their activities.[205] Jephthah forms an exception to this, but he is the exception which proves the rule, for had the other judges taken the lead in military expeditions, these, just as Jephthah's war with the Ammonites, would have been handed down in the tradition. Furthermore, even with Jephthah it is by no means certain that it was in his capacity as judge that he undertook the war with the Ammonites. Since this exploit is narrated before the notice of Jephthah's having 'judged Israel', it would seem to have been the intention of the editor to indicate that in his belief Jephthah did not fight as judge, but became judge after his victory over the Ammonites. So, if the Jephthah tradition is to be ruled out there is no support for the view that leadership in war belonged to the functions of these judges. On the other hand, it is clear from the fact that Samuel made an annual circuit that the functions of the judge were, as the title indicates, judicial in some sense. Further than this, however, it is difficult to go. It is possible that he represented the court of appeal, as the Davidic king did in later time, or that he was the one before whom particularly difficult cases were brought, which is the picture given by Deut. 17.8ff. On the other hand, the judge may also, on ceremonial occasions, have proclaimed law in the assemblies of the people, whether casuistic or apodictic law or both.[206] What is clear, however, is that there is no indication that the judge occupied an office of significance for all Israel, and so there is nothing here which will provide any support for the theory of the amphictyony or which will presuppose the existence of conditions in the period of the judges favourable to the theory of an amphictyony in Israel. The judge was a local official; he had the jurisdiction of a limited area, and was probably appointed by the tribal elders for the judicial administration of that area.[207] The existence of such an official certainly does not demand the existence of an amphictyony.

D. *The Tribal Borders*

It has been suggested[208] that a function of the judges of the list in Judg. 10 and 12 was that of deciding and fixing the borders between the tribes. Although it is doubtful that Josh. 17.14ff. provides any support for this view,[209] and quite apart from the question of whether or not it was precisely these judges who were responsible for determining the tribal boundaries, the problem of the origin of the boundary descriptions now to be found in Josh. 13–19 is of some importance for the subject here under discussion. Its importance lies particularly in the fact that it has been proposed[210] that these boundary descriptions derive from the period of the judges in Israel. If this can be demonstrated, then it will provide some support for the theory of the existence of an Israelite amphictyony; for an established border system such as this presupposes the existence of some form of central authority which would have been able to decide border disputes between the various tribes and to impose decisions and thus fix definite boundaries.

While it is true that the burden of proof lies on those who propose this theory, it is also true that the theory cannot be dismissed on the basis of the statement that there is as yet no conclusive evidence of the existence of a central authority which could have formulated such boundaries.[211] It has already been pointed out[212]

that the evidence in favour of the existence of the Israelite amphictyony is circumstantial; so all the evidence must be taken into
account. If the border system can be shown to derive from the
period of the judges, then the existence of a central authority must
be assumed, and this in turn would constitute some evidence in
favour of the existence of an amphictyony; if this cannot be shown,
then the theory is further weakened. Therefore, judgment on the
time of origin of the border system cannot be delivered on the basis
of a preconceived conclusion on the question of the amphictyony.

Nor can a conclusion be reached on the date of origin of the
border system on the basis of arguments on the time of final editing of these chapters of Joshua. It has been argued[213] that official
material, such as that found in Josh. 13–19, could not have survived
the ransacking of Jerusalem in 587 BC, and that, consequently,
Josh. 13–19 must derive from a post-exilic author, probably the
priestly writer. However, the survival of such official documents
from pre-exilic times is adequately attested by the many references
in the Books of Kings to the Chronicles of the kings of Israel and
Judah. These references presuppose the existence of official records
of the pre-exilic period which have been used in compilations after
587 BC.[214] Thus, the possibility remains open that Josh. 13–19
rests on official, written records deriving from an early time.[215]
The only basis on which to proceed is, then, by general considerations and by an examination of the boundaries themselves.

In the first place, a distinction must be made between two types
of material which have been combined to give the present form of
Josh. 13–19. On the one hand, there are the tribal boundaries
proper, with which we are here specifically concerned; and, on
the other hand, there are the city-lists of Josh. 15.21–62; 18.21–28;
19.2–7, 41–46. These cities are presented as the towns lying within
the territories of the tribes of Judah, Benjamin, Simeon and Dan.
However, the fact that on a number of occasions the same place
is assigned to the territory of more than one tribe[216] leads to the
supposition that these were not originally four different lists, but
represent a secondary splitting up of what was originally a single
list. Moreover, the historical background of such a list, covering
an extended area in the south, can only be the kingdom of Judah.
The list presents those cities which belonged to the kingdom of
Judah at some stage of its history;[217] it may, therefore, be left out
of account at this point.

Yet, when the material which remains is examined, it is clear that it is far from uniform. A comparison between Josh. 15.1–12 and Josh. 19.10–39 will reveal obvious stylistic differences. While Josh. 15.1–12 presents a true description of the border of the tribe of Judah, there is no true border description in Josh. 19.10–39. The latter passage certainly aims at giving the borders of Zebulun, Issachar, Asher and Naphtali, but it is doubtful if this is an original aim. Quite extensive additions have been made to the numbers of towns listed in these verses,[218] but even after these additions have been removed it is unlikely that what remains constitutes genuine border descriptions. The comparison with Josh. 15.1–12 would suggest, rather, that basic to Josh. 19.10–39 there is a list of place names in the manner of those which are provided for Judah in Josh. 15.21–62; 18.21–28; 19.2–7, 41–46.[219] Only at a secondary stage of its history was this list worked up and supplied with a connecting text in order to make it resemble the border description given for Judah in Josh. 15.1–12. The alternative explanation,[220] that all the present border descriptions go back ultimately to lists of fixed border points which were only later supplied with a connecting text, still leaves the difficulty that in their present form clear differences in style are to be seen between the border description of Judah in Josh. 15.1–12 and that given for Zebulun, Issachar, Asher and Naphtali in Josh. 19.10–39. Moreover, since a sharp distinction is made between city-list and border description for Judah, while no such sharp distinction is made for the other tribes in Josh. 19.10–39, it is hard to account for the stylistic differences between the two simply by saying that the Galilean tribes were not the main interest of an editor who supplied the connecting text.[221] It seems preferable, therefore, to understand Josh. 19.10–39 as having originally been a city-list which at a secondary stage was supplied with a connecting text in order to turn it into a border description, and thus harmonize it with other border descriptions which had never existed simply as lists of cities, nor as lists of fixed border points; then, by the same or a later editor, Josh. 19.10–39 was further supplemented through the addition of more cities, apparently derived from Josh. 21 and Judg. 1.

In Josh. 13.15–31 a picture is presented similar to that in Josh. 19. 10-39, in that here also no attempt is made to distinguish between city-lists and border descriptions.[222] Just as in Josh. 19, so also in Josh. 13 no true border descriptions are to be found in the

manner of Josh. 15.1–12. Quite apart from this, however, it is
clear that the territory assigned to Reuben, Gad and half the tribe
of Manasseh in Josh. 13 is no original allotment. In its delineation
of separate areas for Reuben and Gad, and in its presentation of the
relationship between Gad and Gilead, and Machir and Gilead,
Josh. 13 shows itself to be a secondary construction over against
other geographical statements of the Old Testament, especially
Num. 32, in which Reuben and Gad are regularly taken together
and in which Gilead was settled by Machir alone.[223] So Josh.
13.15–31 may also be left out of consideration here.

The passages which remain relevant in the present connection
are Josh. 15.1–12; 16.1–3, 5–8; 17.7–10; 18.11–20. Although the
substantial repetition of Josh. 16.1–3 in 16.5b–6a may in fact be
the result of the former having been originally the northern border
of the kingdom of Judah rather than the southern border of the
house of Joseph,[224] these sections still constitute genuine border
descriptions for Judah, Ephraim, Manasseh and Benjamin.
Further, there are a number of points which encourage confidence
in the originality and reality of these border descriptions. In the
first place, such borders are provided for only four tribes. It is only
when these are taken along with the other city-lists that the aim of
describing the settlement areas of all the tribes is attained. If Josh.
13–19 as a whole were the work of an editor, the result would have
been a uniform plan of the division of the land among the tribes.
Secondly, the twists and turns of the borders as they are described
for the four tribes also supports the view that they reflect real
conditions of settlement. A comparison with the artificial division
of the land among the tribes in Ezek. 48.1–29 clearly demon-
strates that the border descriptions of the Book of Joshua are
based on conditions as these existed after settlement in the land.[225]
Thus, the editor of these chapters is not the author of the information which is contained in them, but is dependent on tradition – tradition which, moreover, was most probably written.
Thirdly, there is positive indication that these borders reflect conditions of early post-settlement times, or at least of a time before
the administrative division of the kingdom by Solomon.[226] Thus,
Josh. 17.9 notes that although the land around the city of Tappuah
belonged to Manasseh, the city itself belonged to Ephraim. This
reflects conditions of the time when Manasseh established itself
as an independent tribe to the north of Ephraim.[227] Similarly, Josh.

15.8 pushes the northern border of Judah right up to the edge of Jerusalem, thus cutting that city off from its territory in the plain of Rephaim. This again seems to reflect the early occupation by Judah of this area which had belonged to the city-state of Jerusalem.

However, another feature of these borders is that they include areas which were certainly not occupied by the Israelite tribes before the rise of the monarchy. The settlement of the Israelite tribes in Palestine in the main affected only the mountain areas at first, while the coastal plain and the plain of Megiddo, where the main concentrations of Canaanite city-states were to be found, were left untouched. It was only in the time of David, when Israel was on the road to becoming a territorial rather than a national state that those parts of the land west of Jordan which Israel had not conquered at the time of settlement were incorporated within Israel.[228] However, the territory of those tribes for whom borders are supplied is given as extending over those areas not settled by Israel at first. Thus, the western boundary of Judah is the coastline of the Mediterranean (Josh. 15.12), and so also is that of Ephraim (Josh. 16.6, 8) and of Manasseh (Josh. 17.9), while the case was probably the same in the original boundary description given for the tribe of Benjamin.[229] Thus, the clear aim of this border system is to treat all the land west of Jordan as Israelite, and so to leave none of it unassigned in the division of the land among the tribes.

In that the coastal plain is divided among the tribes, this system cannot be understood to be based on historical conditions of the immediate post-settlement period. The points which connect the border system with actual conditions which came into existence as an immediate result of the settlement of the tribes have already been noted; as well as this, the further point has been made[230] that the incorporation of hitherto non-Israelite areas into Israel in the time of David would have meant that these non-Israelite areas would have been reckoned as part of the state of Israel and would not have been considered as territory to be assigned to individual tribes – yet it is precisely to the individual tribes that this territory is assigned in the boundary system in Joshua. On this basis, then, it has been proposed[231] that the border system is founded on a combination of claim and reality and comes from the period of the judges. It is based on reality in that it faithfully reflects the actual areas settled by the individual tribes; and it is based on claim in that it adds to these areas further territory which as yet the tribes did not possess but which they nevertheless claimed that they should possess. No distinction is made between real and claimed possession in the boundary descriptions; this is simply because the whole land west of Jordan is considered as Israelite, whether or not Israel has actually managed to settle all of it, and as such it is to be distributed among the various tribes.

However, this theory is made especially doubtful by the fact that the boundary descriptions themselves do not deal with the whole land west of the Jordan. For Issachar certainly, and probably also for the other three Galilean tribes mentioned in Josh. 19, there are no original boundary descriptions. Instead, there are here basically city-lists, and it is first through the editorial combination of these with the boundary descriptions that all of west Jordan is covered. Nor indeed is any real northern boundary given for the tribe of Manasseh. The extent of its territory in the north is given in Josh. 17.10 simply by reference to the other tribes which bordered on it. Even the northern border of Ephraim and the southern border of Manasseh in Josh. 16.8; 17.7–9 are indicated in very vague and general terms compared with the detailed descriptions of the boundaries of Benjamin and Judah. In fact, it may be said that the border system as such is really concerned in a detailed way with the southern part of west Jordan, taking in Judah and Benjamin, and Ephraim only in so far as it affected the southern area. This does not sound like a plan drawn up within the context of an Israelite amphictyony in the period of the judges recording decisions on how all of west Jordan should be divided among the tribes. Furthermore, the view that, in giving the Mediterranean coastline as the western boundary of several tribes, the boundary system is based on a combination of real land possessions and claimed possessions, is not the only explanation possible. The inclusion of these areas not at first settled by the tribes could very well rest on the actual extent of Israelite territory in the monarchy period. The objection that in such a case this originally non-Israelite territory would not have been reckoned as the territory of individual tribes but would have been thought of as territory belonging to the state of Israel, is not really of much force. For given the religious significance of the land as Israel's heritage,[232] it is clear that the distribution of all this land by Joshua among the tribes is an essential conclusion of the narrative in the first half of the Book of Joshua which deals with the conquest of all the land by the united Israelite tribes under the leadership of Joshua. The boundary system may be seen on the one hand as a realization of how things should have been in the period immediately following the settlement, and on the other hand as a justification of how things had come to be in the period of the monarchy. It is not to be imagined that the rise of the monarchy signalled the immediate end of tribal consciousness and of interest in tribal territory. It was only gradually, as a result of such events as Solomon's administrative division of the kingdom which in part disregarded tribal divisions, and as a result of the division of the kingdom after the death of Solomon, that distinct tribal boundaries would have lost their significance. David may have conquered large areas of west Jordan which the tribes had not succeeded in settling, but this was simply a realization of the intention of Yahweh for the tribes of Israel. In the light of this, it appears very likely that the boundary system does come from the time of the early monarchy, and that it is based, on the one hand, on the actual territory which the individual tribes had long occupied, and, on the other hand, on the assignment to the tribes of other areas incorporated within Israel by David. Moreover, this period forms a better background than does any Israelite amphictyony for the fact that the boundary system is really concerned only with the southern part of the country. It may be considered as a product of the Judean part of David's empire, which, beginning in the time of David himself, gradually came to constitute a separate entity within the kingdom until the formal division of the kingdom after the death of Solomon;[233] the boundary system is interested only in that part of west Jordan which falls within the southern area, and deals with other territory only in so far as this touches on the southern area.[234] It was only later, as a result of editorial activity which combined city-lists with this boundary system, that the picture of territory assigned to all twelve tribes came into existence.

E. *War in the Period of the Judges*

The Israelite amphictyony has been described as a 'band of tribes which, besides engaging in cultic activities in the narrower sense, also safeguarded and defended its whole political existence, sword in hand'.[235] Although it is true that in Greece in later time the

member states of the amphictyony presented anything but a united
front against the Persian invader Xerxes,[236] and so a similar lack
of unity among the Israelite tribes cannot be taken to disprove the
existence of an amphictyony, yet it is still the case that it is only
to be expected that on occasions the combined forces of the tribes
should have appeared in battle; moreover, if the tribes did appear
together in battle one may assume that conditions favourable to
the existence of an amphictyony were present.

Since our concern here is with the period during which an
amphictyony is supposed to have existed in Israel, that is, from
the conclusion of the settlement of the tribes through the period
of the judges, the event of the actual settlement itself lies strictly
outside our frame of reference. This is fortunate since it is a subject which demands a much more thorough treatment than could
be devoted to it at this point.[237] However, whether one is to
think of a gradual, largely peaceful infiltration of the land by semi-
nomads, within the context of a seasonal change of pasture, or of
a more concerted bloody onslaught by Israelite tribes on the former inhabitants of the land, this will not decide the question of
the existence of an Israelite amphictyony. The latter is supposed
to have been established only after the settlement had taken place,
whatever pre-settlement connections may have existed between
the tribes, and Josh. 24 has been taken as its 'foundation charter'.[238]
So it is to the battles which the tradition places in the time between
the settlement of the tribes in the land and the rise of the monarchy
that attention must be directed in order to find some manifestation
of a unity among the tribes which would support the theory that
the Israelite tribes were banded together in an amphictyony.

Two further points which, since they only slightly impinge on
our problem, need not be discussed in detail, may be briefly
mentioned. The first of these concerns the character and nature of
war in the period of the judges. Because of the way in which these
wars were conducted they are commonly referred to as 'holy
wars'.[239] While this is perhaps not the most suitable designation
for them,[240] it may continue to be used despite its limitations,
since it does convey some idea of the sacral nature of the events
described. It is, however, impossible to be certain on exactly what
was involved in the conduct of a holy war. Quite apart from
questions such as the degree to which ritual sanctification and
abstention were required on the part of the warriors involved in

the battle,[241] the various traditions dealing with the holy wars reveal more fundamental discrepancies.[242] Thus, for example, the tradition in some places speaks of the spirit of Yahweh coming on the one designated to lead the holy war, while in other places, instead of this there is a more extensive prelude to the account of the actual war, which tells of enquiry being made of Yahweh and of Yahweh's answer. In many of these differences one should undoubtedly see the formative influence of circles of traditionists,[243] each of which has given its own presentation to the traditions which it has handed down. However, the difficulties to which this gives rise when it comes to determining what a holy war was and how it was conducted,[244] need not detain us at this point. Our immediate purpose is to see the extent to which the tribes of Israel were involved in any one action.

The second preliminary point is, however, of somewhat more relevance and importance. This has to do with a distinction which has been made between holy war and amphictyonic war.[245] Such a distinction has been prompted by a number of factors: the Old Testament is silent on the amphictyony while it has much to say about the holy war; the amphictyony does not appear in the holy war; the commissioning of the leader of the holy war does not come from the amphictyony but from Yahweh;[246] there is no original connection between such amphictyonic institutions as the judge of Israel[247] and the central sanctuary[248] on the one hand, and the holy war on the other. Holy war and amphictyony are two originally distinct institutions; the former had its origin with the Rachel tribes coming out of Egypt, while the latter belongs with the Leah group of tribes which were at this time already settled in the land.[249] The two were gradually fused, and the original distinction between them consequently became blurred on account of the settlement of the Rachel tribes in the land, their becoming members of the amphictyony, and the God of the holy war (Yahweh) being accepted by the Leah tribes as the God of the amphictyony.[250]

If it is true that this distinction should be made, that the holy war has little or no bearing on the question of the existence of an amphictyony,[251] this will clearly have considerable relevance to the subject with which we are concerned here. It means simply that even if all the tribes of Israel cannot be shown to have taken part in a particular action this does not cast doubt on the possibility of the existence of an amphictyony. On the other hand, however, if it can be shown that all the tribes did act together, this, as we said earlier, will stand in favour of an amphictyonic connection of the tribes.

Judges 3 tells of three occasions in which Israel was oppressed and then delivered. The events described – the defeat of Cushan-rishathaim by Othniel, the defeat of Eglon by Ehud, and the defeat of the Philistines by Shamgar – stand at present in a context which shows all Israel to have been involved; it is Israel which is oppressed and Israel which is delivered. However, this context is a contribution of the editorial framework,252 which has given a national significance to what were originally quite local traditions; that is, traditions which originally dealt with events in which only a very limited group was involved have now been taken up into the history of Israel as a whole and accepted as a record of the events which concerned the whole people. It is, therefore, only after disregarding this framework that there exists the possibility of determining the original reference of these traditions. Apart from this framework in the Othniel tradition (Judg. 3.7–11) there are, however, only the proper names of Othniel and Cushan-rishathaim. The latter name is otherwise unknown, and since his oppression of Israel is recorded solely within the framework passage there seems little hope of discovering how it is that the tradition has preserved his name. The name Othniel is to be found elsewhere in Josh. 15.16–19 and Judg. 1.12–15. If the same individual (or clan) is meant in all these passages, then it may be assumed with some degree of probability that the intention behind Judg. 3.7–11 is to provide for Judah (Othniel being the ancestor of a clan of the Kenizzites, a tribe of Judah) a charismatic deliverer. None of the other deliverers came from Judah.253

With the tradition on Ehud, however, it is possible to be more definite. Again without the framework, this tradition records a dispute between the tribe of Benjamin and the Moabites, in which the tribe of Ephraim was also later involved. It may not perhaps be possible to clarify all the background details of this event, but its local significance is nevertheless quite clear.

Judges 3.31 represents a unique tradition. It is unique in that it celebrates a non-Israelite defeat of the Philistines as a victory for Israel. Shamgar, the son of Anath, by his name and parentage was a Canaanite chieftain.254 That his victory over the Philistines should have come to be included as part of Israel's history is probably due simply to Israel's view of the Philistines as their eternal enemies; the defeat of the Philistines, no matter by whom, was a victory and a deliverance for Israel. At any rate, there is no question here of an Israelite amphictyony in action or presupposed in the background.

From this point we may pass on to a brief consideration of the Gideon tradition in Judg. 6–8 from the same point of view.[255] This tradition presents many difficulties, particularly in connection with the relationship between Gideon and Jerubbaal, but a treatment of these is not necessary at this point.[256] That section of the narrative which is relevant here is to be found in Judg. 6.33–8.3. Judges 8.4–21, which presents many parallels to the preceding section, has simply a blood feud as its subject. However, in the tradition of Gideon's battle with the Midianites, in Judg. 6.33–8.3, even if it is taken exactly for what it says, there is no question of all Israel's having been involved at any stage of the action. Furthermore, it is highly unlikely that all those tribes which are specifically mentioned were concerned. Judges 6.35 records that Manasseh, Asher, Zebulun and Naphtali were summoned to battle. These were reduced to three hundred men who actually carried out the attack on the Midianite camp, after which, according to Judg. 7.23, Naphtali, Asher and Manasseh, and, according to 7.24, Ephraim, were called out in pursuit of Midian. However, Judg. 8.2 would suggest that, apart from the clan of Abiezer to which Gideon belonged, the only tribe involved in this exploit was Ephraim, and that at a late stage, just as in the Ehud tradition.[257] The explicit addition of the other tribes may have arisen because of their proximity to the site of the Midianite camp, the valley of Jezreel, or, after the connection of this tradition with Judg. 8.4–21, because of the reference in 8.18 to Mount Tabor which seems to have been the site of an important sanctuary on the border of Zebulun and Naphtali.[258] Once again, there is no hint of amphictyonic action in this episode, nor does Gideon's undertaking presuppose the existence of any amphictyony.

In the same way, the kingship which Abimelech held at Shechem had nothing to do with any federation of tribes. He was made king by the citizens of Shechem (Judg. 9.6), and not by any tribe; his monarchy, like that offered to Gideon/Jerubbaal before him, was of limited extent only, and probably involved the city of Shechem alone with perhaps also its surrounding villages. As such, it should be seen in the light of kingship as this was exercised by the kings of the Canaanite city-states, rather than in the light of the later Israelite monarchy.[259] There is no quesion of an amphictyonic Israel in action here.

The same conclusion must be drawn for the tradition of the defeat of the Ammonites by the Gileadite Jephthah. The threatening appearance of the Ammonites on their border[260] forced the Gileadites to hire Jephthah to defend them. Since it is only Gileadites who take any active part in the battle, Judg. 10.9 cannot be used to show that a much wider coalition of tribes was involved.[261] Once again, this was originally a purely local Gileadite tradition, though probably different from the other traditions of charismatic deliverers in that Jephthah seems to have been a freebooter just hired for the occasion,[262] which has now been set within a framework giving the event significance for all Israel.

Compared with those traditions in the Book of Judges which have already been mentioned, the Samson stories were probably brought into their present position at a relatively late stage.[263] In spite of this, however, they are basically very old traditon; they presuppose the presence of the tribe of Dan in the area bordering on Philistine territory, to the west of the territory occupied by the tribe of Benjamin, and thus tell of a period before the Danites migrated to their final place of settlement in the north (Judg. 18). These Samson stories tell of no great victory achieved by Israel over their enemies, nor is Samson said to have been raised up by Yahweh in order to deliver Israel from oppression in the same way that this is related of the other charismatic deliverers;[264] yet the tradition is now set within the framework of Israel's having sinned and having been given into the power of the Philistines. However, in so far as the tradition does tell of conflict with the Philistines, this conflict is simply of the nature of border disputes. Samson led no army against the Philistines, and the only tribe besides that of Dan which appears in the story, and that in a very minor way, is Judah. So once again, there is no hint of the existence of an amphictyony in this tradition.

So far, then, there has been no evidence of a united appearance of the Israelite tribes in battle which could provide support for the theory of an amphictyonic connection of the Israelite tribes in the period of the judges. If the existence of an amphictyony is presupposed for this period it would perhaps be legitimate to argue that the call for help by one tribe to another, which is to be found on a number of occasions,[265] attests a feeling of unity which must be understood within the context of the amphictyony. However, an amphictyony is certainly not an essential presupposition for understanding this feeling of unity, especially since, in those episodes which have been considered, help was sought from only one tribe apart from the tribe which was directly involved. So far, therefore, the most that can be established is that there was a feeling of kinship between Benjamin and Ephraim (Judg. 3.27), the Abiezrites and Ephraim (Judg. 7.24), and between Gilead and Ephraim (Judg. 12.1f.). This does not constitute the sort of unity for which we are looking at this point.

The events which have been dealt with up until now have been battles in which Israelite tribes engaged in order to alleviate oppression from an outside group. We now turn to an event of a very different kind in which there is no external oppressor;[266] this is the war between Benjamin and the rest of the Israelite tribes, recorded in Judg. 19–21. The literary-critical problems of these chapters have already been mentiond,[267] and so we may proceed immediately to a treatment of the significance of the tradition.

The appearance in these chapters of vocabulary which is used otherwise mainly in late texts, together with the fact that in this tradition Israel is shown as a centralized, ecclesiastical assembly, rather than as a political community, would seem to indicate the late composition of the narrative. However, this vocabulary is regarded by Noth as part of the stock language of the amphictyony, which appears in the tradition of Judg. 19–21 particularly because this is one of the few direct amphictyonic traditions preserved in the Old Testament.[268] Its subject is the punishment meted out by the members of the amphictyony to a fellow-member, Benjamin, for a breach of amphictyonic law – an episode which is closely paralleled in Greek history, in a war waged by the amphictyony against the Locrians in 339 BC for a breach of amphictyonic law committed by the city of Amphissa.[269]

That this parallel may stand involves a quite literal acceptance of the tradition of Judg. 19–21 after it has been subjected to literary criticism: as a result of a crime committed against a Levite and his concubine by the men of Gibeah, a city of Benjamin, a war of punishment was declared against Benjamin by the rest of the tribes of the amphictyony. It is very doubtful, however, if this interpretation can stand up to scrutiny. There are two questions which must be posed: firstly, what tribes were involved; and, secondly, what was the subject of the dispute.

There are two points which support the idea that all the Israelite tribes were involved in the event: in the first place, there is the account of how the Levite divided his concubine into twelve pieces which he sent through all Israel (Judg. 19.29). However, it is unlikely that this obvious reference to the twelve tribes of Israel formed an original part of the tradition. Quite apart from the fact that a piece would scarcely have been sent to Benjamin, the phrase 'into twelve pieces' should be omitted on literary-critical grounds, as an unsuitable antecedent to the object of 'sent' in the following phrase;[270] in view of the parallel formula in I Sam. 11.7 also, it is unlikely that a reference to 'twelve pieces' formed part of the original text in Judg. 19. The other support for the involvement of all the tribes is to be found in the general references in Judg. 20.1f. to 'all the people of Israel', and 'the chiefs of all the people, of all the tribes of Israel' who gathered at Mizpah. However, the unreliability of these expressions, at least in the present context, is immediately clear from the fact that Judg. 20.3, 12ff make it obvious that Benjamin was not present at this gathering.

The only other method which can be used to determine which tribes took part in the action is to see which tribes are explicitly mentioned as taking part in what can be reconstructed of the original narrative. Certainly, it is not enough to rely on Judg. 20.10 for the conjecture that the tradition knew of the existence of a federation of ten tribes on this occasion, just because the number ten happens to be used as the basis for the formation of an army;[271] the procedure must be to find out precisely which tribes were involved in the original tradition in this 'amphictyonic' action against Benjamin.

Apart from Benjamin itself, there are only three tribes specifically mentioned in the tradition: Gilead, Judah and Ephraim, and it is unlikely that even all of these belonged to the original story. Gilead is named specifically in Judg. 20.1, but since it otherwise appears only in the two interwoven aetiological traditions in Judg. 21.1ff., which came late to their present context,[272] it is a reasonable assumption that the reference to Gilead in Judg. 20.1 is also a late addition introduced in anticipation of the place which it was to occupy in the aetiological ending of the narrative. Judah figures in a dual capacity in the tradition: first, as the tribe in which lay the city of Bethlehem, the home town of the Levite's concubine. However, in addition to the fact that this is probably a late element which has been brought not only into this tradition but also into the preceding one in Judg. 17–18,[273] it does not really constitute an integral connection between Judah and the action undertaken against Benjamin. Secondly, in Judg. 20.18 Judah appears as the tribe which was commanded to go up first against Benjamin. However, it was noted earlier[274] that since this command is quite unsuitable in its context, and since it is not fulfilled anyway, this verse must be judged an addition taken from Judg. 1.1f. Ephraim, however, is integral to the tradition: the Levite dwelt in Ephraim (Judg. 19.1); it was an Ephraimite living in Gibeah who gave the Levite hospitality (Jud. 19.16). So it seems probable that Judg. 19–21 preserves a tradition which told originally of a dispute involving only two tribes, Ephraim and Benjamin. As with the other traditions with which we have dealt so far, it was only at a subsequent stage that this local dispute assumed significance for all Israel in the tradition.

If this is accepted it casts serious doubt on the validity of the parallel which has been drawn between this tradition and an event of Greek amphictyonic history. Not only does no amphictyony appear in the Israelite tradition, but also there is no indication of the exclusion of Benjamin from such an amphictyony, which was the penalty which the Locrians brought on themselves for the breach of amphictyonic law committed by their city Amphissa.

This leads on to the second of the two questions posed above: the real subject of the dispute between Ephraim and Benjamin. Did the tribe of Benjamin offend against 'amphictyonic' law? The tradition told of an assault by the men of Gibeah on a Levite's concubine. Because this Levite was living in Ephraim his welfare was the responsibility of that tribe, and so, on the refusal of the tribe of Benjamin to hand over the criminals, a war of punishment was undertaken by Ephraim against Benjamin. However, since it seems unlikely that the whole tribe of Benjamin would have supported the men of Gibeah in such a crime, and since in a number of places in the Old Testament the motif of a sexual offence is used in order to justify or explain a particular action or state,[275] it is worth asking if something different in the relations between Ephraim and Benjamin lies behind the tradition of Judg. 19–21.

If the tradition of Judg. 19–21 does conceal a different event it is possible to make a reasonable conjecture on the nature of it. The tribe of Ephraim occupies a prominent position throughout the Book of Judges. In Judg. 8.1ff.; 12.1ff. Gideon and Jephthah are upbraided by Ephraimites for their failure to summon them to battle; in Judg. 3.15ff. Ephraim is called out to help Benjamin in the battle against Moab initiated by a Benjaminite; Ephraim is the first tribe specifically mentioned in the Song of Deborah (Judg. 5.14). Furthermore, there are several hints that a special relationship existed between Ephraim and Benjamin. This is indicated not only by the tradition in Judg. 19-21, and by the Ehud tradition in Judg. 3, and by the close association of these two tribes in the Song of Deborah (Judg. 5.14), but also by the fact that it is an Ephraimite, Joshua, who plays the major role in what is understood by many to be the conquest tradition of Benjamin in Josh. 2-9.[276] There are a number of further considerations. We saw earlier[277] that there is no reference to Benjamin in the story of the birth of the sons of Jacob in Gen. 29-30, and this tribe seems also to be ignored in the early part of the story of Joseph in Gen. 37. There is, however, a particular tradition of the birth of Benjamin to Rachel in the land of Palestine in Gen. 35.16ff. The final point to be noted is the meaning of the name Benjamin – 'sons of the south'. This name would indicate that at some particular time, probably at the time of origin of the group bearing this name, this group lived to the south of some prominent neighbour or in the southern part of some district.[278] On this basis, then, there is good foundation for the theory that the tribe of Benjamin originated in the land of Palestine as a split-off from the tribe of Ephraim after the settlement.[279] Benjamin would thus have formed a particular group within Ephraim and would have lived in the southern part of the area occupied by Ephraim. It was a warlike group, and the Ehud tradition would indicate that it was capable of acting on its own, without reference to the rest of Ephraim. If this is the background against which the tradition of Judg. 19-21 must be seen, it is possible that this tradition makes concealed reference to one stage in the process at the end of which Benjamin came to stand as a completely independent tribe on an equal footing with the other tribes. The event to which reference is made here, however, is an unsuccessful attempt[280] by Benjamin to free itself of the dominance of Ephraim and establish its independence; this state was not attained until a later time.

It must be admitted that this reconstruction is very uncertain; but if it is true, then as far as Judg. 19–21 is concerned there is no question of an amphictyonic war against Benjamin being recorded here, nor was there any transgression of amphictyonic law by Benjamin. However, even if this background cannot be maintained, it still remains the case that Judg. 19–21 originally told of a dispute involving Ephraim and Benjamin only; furthermore, even if this tradition is accepted simply for what it says in the matter of the nature and cause of the dispute, the presupposition of the existence of an amphictyony is of no particular help for our appreciation of the reason for the action of Ephraim.

Our conclusion for this section must be, therefore, that if it can be shown that an amphictyony existed in Israel in the period of the judges there is no particular difficulty raised by the traditions which we have been considering. On the other hand, however, these traditions themselves provide no support whatever for the theory of the existence of an Israelite amphictyony.

ISRAEL IN THE PERIOD OF THE JUDGES

The period before the rise of Saul still remains obscure. So far we have emphasized what did not exist at this time: there is no evidence of any central authority, nor, in those traditions we have examined, of any communal activity by the tribes of Israel which would support the view that conditions favourable to the existence of an amphictyony were present. However, it is possible to balance this rather negative picture with something more positive. It is impossible to agree that Israel in the period of the judges was organized along the lines of the Greek amphictyonies of a later age, but an attempt can nevertheless be made to outline the nature of the divisions which separated the tribes and to trace the stages in the process by which the tribes eventually came to form an active unit. This does not imply that the tribes, at least as far as Judah and Ephraim are concerned, had nothing in common until the time of the foundation of the state; for, as we saw at the beginning of this book, it is highly unlikely that the existence of the entity called 'Israel' can be accounted for satisfactorily from the period of the monarchy, from the time of Saul on. At the moment, all that is implied is that the period of the judges was for Israel a period of divisions in which, by force of circumstances, communal action either in politics or in cult was impossible. This indeed is the general picture presented by the Book of Judges itself when its schematic framework is disregarded, which can therefore be taken as an accurate reflection of the period with which it is concerned.

Against this background, the Song of Deborah in Judg. 5 stands out as a notable exception to the rule that the traditions of the Book of Judges present Israel as a collection of wholly disunited tribes. The Song is notable for two reasons: in the first place, it is a very ancient piece of poetry; but, secondly, and more important in the present context, it commemorates the only occasion known to us in this time when it is difficult to deny that a wide alliance of tribes took part in a concerted action. Naturally, since the Song of Deborah is unique in this respect, it has been subjected to much attention over the past years; but in spite of this no generally agreed conclusions have been reached on many aspects of its significance. However, of the many questions which are most disputed,[1] there are only two which must be discussed here; these are, first, the situation out of which the Song arose, and secondly, the date of the event commemorated in the Song.

In the matter of the background of the Song of Deborah the point in which we are primarily interested is whether the tribes mentioned in Judg. 5.14–18 are addressed as participants and non-participants in the battle against Sisera; that is to say, are some tribes praised for taking part in the battle and others reprimanded for staying away, or are they being addressed in some other connection?

Our task has been defined in the form of this question in view especially of a quite recent interpretation which has been proposed for the Song of Deborah.[2] According to this interpretation, the Song had a cultic *Sitz im Leben*; it formed a liturgical component of a festival of covenant renewal.[3] In this festival the tribal federation called 'Israel' and the victorious battle troops participate in order to celebrate not only the defeat of Sisera but also their sacral unity as the people of Yahweh. The phrase 'to the gates' in Judg. 5.11b refers, not to the gates of the places where the warriors lived, nor to the gates of the enemy cities, but to the gates of the place where the festival was celebrated, which may have been on Mount Tabor. This mountain, as the meeting point of the borders of three tribes, Issachar, Naphtali and Zebulun, was the gathering place of the troops under Barak before the battle,[4] and would thus have been the place to which they returned to celebrate their victory in the context of a covenant festival. In the following verses (Judg. 5.12ff.) there is a ceremonial procession of the people of Yahweh, which is initiated by a signal from Deborah. It is this signal which Deborah is called on to give in v. 12. This means that in the following vv. 14–17 the tribes which are mentioned are those which sent representatives to this cultic festival and those which did not do so; these verses do not refer to the participants and non-participants in the battle against Sisera. The account of the actual battle does not begin until v. 19, and it is preceded, in v. 18, by a reference to the only two tribes, Zebulun and Naphtali, which had taken part. It is the victory of this limited group which is taken up and celebrated by the wider federation of the tribes. In support of this view the point has also been put forward[5] that attendance at the festival would have been voluntary – hence the light reprimand on the tribes which did not turn up – while participation in the battle would have been obligatory. Absence from the battle would have been punished by a curse of the sort that is pronounced on Meroz (Judg. 5.23), a city which must therefore have belonged to one of the two tribes which had fought the battle.

This interpretation of the Song of Deborah has the advantage that it provides an explanation for the repetition, in v. 18, of the tribes of Zebulun and Naphtali, which have already been mentioned in vv. 14f.,[6] and also for the fact that it is only these two tribes which are explicitly referred to in the narrative of Judg. 4 as having fought against Sisera under Barak. Furthermore, such a cultic background fits very well with the clear hymnic quality of the Song, especially in its introduction and conclusion, for which analogies may be found in several psalms.[7] However, in spite of this, it is unlikely that this is the correct interpretation. There is, indeed, nothing intrinsically impossible in the idea that an event in which only a small group took part should have been celebrated by Israel as a whole as part of her history. Undoubtedly, very few experienced the Exodus from Egypt, but the Old Testament presents this as an event experienced by the ancestors of all Israel. However, just as this view of the Exodus is the result of a long process of transmission and re-interpretation of the Exodus tradition, so also the Song of Deborah as a piece of cultic poetry is the end product of its transmission from the time that the tradition first arose on the basis of the victory over Sisera. In other words, the view that the Song of Deborah is a cultic poem used in the context of cultic worship and praise of Yahweh is valid only for one particular stage of the history of the Song, and that stage is the one which the Song reached just before it was put into its present context in the Old Testament;[8] it does not, on the other hand, provide a satisfactory explanation for the origin and growth of the Song.

One of the points which has been used to give a measure of support to this cultic interpretation is the fact that it explains what appears to be a discrepancy between the Song and the prose version of the battle against Sisera in Judg. 4. According to the latter, only two tribes – Zebulun and Naphtali – took part, while in the Song several other tribes are mentioned. Since, however, this reference to Judg. 4 introduces a point of principle, it is something which must be dealt with before we turn to the Song of Deborah in particular. The principle involves the possibility of making such comparisons between the Song and the prose account in Judg. 4. There are two considerations which should indicate that it is not possible to draw immediate comparisons and contrasts between Judg. 4 and 5: in the first place, the Song in Judg. 5 is composed in poetry while Judg. 4 is in prose; this means, secondly, that the two chapters have come down to us by different routes. The effect of this is that it is only after the prose story and the Song have been investigated quite separately from the point of view of the origin and growth of their traditions, that it is possible to draw any conclusions from a comparison between the two.[9] It is methodically wrong to attempt such comparisons before this investigation has been carried out.

Judges 4 presents a too uneven and inconsistent text for it to be used uncritically to reconstruct the nature of this event.[10] Jabin is said to be the king of Canaan (v. 2), and Sisera his army commander (vv. 2,7); yet Jabin reigned in Hazor, while Sisera dwelt in Harosheth-hagoiim (vv. 2, 13, 16). Furthermore, there was at this time no single political entity called Canaan over which Jabin could have been king, and indeed Jabin plays no part in the actual battle in which the enemies of Israel are led by Sisera alone. Again, there is some confusion as to the place where Barak summoned his troops, whether Tabor (vv. 6, 12, 14) or Kedesh (vv. 9, 10). The inconsistencies so far mentioned are, however, mainly confined to the first part of the chapter, in vv. 1–11. From v. 12 on there is a much more uniform narrative. Yet even here it is possible to make out at least one stage in a development of the tradition. The first part of this section, in vv. 12–16, gives a formalized and rather lifeless account of the battle to which v. 16 is clearly a definite conclusion. On the other hand, from v. 17 on a new scene is set in which the main part is taken by Jael. This is a detailed account of a particular event in which two people speak and act. There is no formal style as with the earlier verses; rather the language is colourful and lively.

This division of the chapter into three sections not only fits the varied styles to be found there, and the inconsistencies noted above, but it also conforms with the broad divisions which may be made in the chapter according to which character plays the chief role. In the first part it is undoubtedly Deborah who is most important, from v. 12 on it is Barak, and from v. 17 it is Jael. But if this is an accurate division, the question is immediately raised if there is any possibility of deciding which of the three sections stands closest to the event which is described and what gave rise to the form of story which is now to be found in the other two sections; or is it to be concluded that all three sections stand equally close to the event with the varied emphases being simply the result of the fact that each section is concerned with a different stage of the battle, while the other points are only minor inconsistencies which came in during the course of transmission of the tradition. There seems no doubt, however, that these sections must be taken as quite distinct, and that the priority should be assigned to the final section, in so far as it stands closest to the event. In these verses there is a straight narrative about a particular event which faithfully describes the details of a certain action; in vv. 12–16, on the other hand, there is a story which is concerned not with describing the event but with treating the event in the light of certain principles and ideas. In particular, this section should be seen as the work of an editor whose presentation of the event is governed wholly by the idea of the holy war: it is Yahweh who takes the lead against Sisera, and it is Yahweh who works deliverance for Israel.[11] This, in that it represents a particular interpretation of the event, would put this section farther from the event than that which follows it.

In the first section of the chapter, not only is there apparently an attempt to exalt Deborah at the expense of Barak, but Jabin is also introduced as king of Canaan reigning in Hazor.[12] It is to this section also that there belong the only two references to Zebulun and Naphtali as the tribes which took part in the battle (vv. 6, 10). Probably this section does contain old tradition, as in the reference to Tabor in v. 6; on the other hand, however, the explicit references to Jabin and to Zebulun and Naphtali most likely derive from another tradition. In Josh. 11.1–15 there is a tradition of the defeat of Jabin and the destruction of Hazor by Israel under the command of Joshua. In distinction to many of the earlier stories of the Book of Joshua which must be judged as aetiological, this tradition is basically a historical war narrative dealing with the defeat of Jabin by some Israelite tribes.[13] In its present form it is a tradition of all Israel, and, as with the earlier stories in Joshua, it has been given this form so that it might fit with the conception of a united conquest of Palestine by Israel under Joshua. Originally, however, this Hazor tradition probably told of a conquest by a more limited group carried out either in the course of settlement or in the course of expansion of their territory. Since Hazor lay in Galilee, the tribes which come into consideration here are the Galilean tribes, especially Zebulun and Naphtali. It is, then, to this separate tradition of the conquest of Hazor that Jabin, Zebulun and Naphtali originally belong, and not to the tradition of the defeat of Sisera by Barak. How it happened that a confusion of these traditions took place is not so clear, but it is probable that it was because these two tribes had taken part in both events and because the traditions of both were handed on at the same place – at the sanctuary on Tabor.

As far as Judg. 4 is concerned, then, it is evident that its earliest component is its final section in vv. 17a, 18–22, or at least it is this section which stands closest to the event. While the event recounted here must always have had some setting in tradition, this setting is now handed down only in an edited version in the preceding two sections, which have been edited according to particular ideas and which have drawn in material from different traditions, and which, consequently, can only be used in the broadest outline for a reconstruction of the context of the action of Jael.

To return to the Song of Deborah, our investigation of Judg. 4 yields the result that this chapter cannot be used in support of the cultic interpretation of the Song of Deborah which has been proposed. Whether or not Zebulun and Naphtali were the only two tribes which fought against Sisera is a question on its own which cannot be decided by appeal to the narrative of Judg. 4. However, this question cannot be answered with any degree of certainty unless an investigation of this Song is carried out similar to that which was applied to Judg. 4. As with the latter, so also the Song has grown to its present form, and only when this growth is understood will it be possible to reach a satisfactory interpretation of the Song.[14]

As a start, it may be noted that the cultic language of the Song, with its description of a theophany and its summons to praise Yahweh,[15] is really confined to the introduction to the Song and to its conclusion; it is only here that the psalmodic style is quite evident. On the other hand, the kernel of the Song is not expressed in this cultic style; there is nothing in it reminiscent of the language used in the festival cult, and unlike the introduction and conclusion, no linguistic and conceptual parallels can be drawn between this part of the Song and the psalms.[16] This linguistic observation fits perfectly with the contrast which may be drawn also between the content of the introduction and conclusion of the Song on the one hand and the content of its kernel on the other. The introduction to the Song, in vv.2–11, and its conclusion, in v.31, are directed towards Yahweh: through the reference to the theophany of Yahweh in vv.4–5, and to his 'triumphs' in v.11, the event which is commemorated has been turned into a deliverance wrought for Israel by Yahweh, which is to be celebrated in festival song in a cultic context. On the other hand, the kernel of the Song, in vv.12–30, has a quite different concern and emphasis.[17] Here it is not Yahweh who is praised, nor is it Yahweh who is addressed; the concern of this part of the Song is with the individual tribes, some of which are praised while others are reprimanded; from this point the Song passes directly on to a description of the battle against Sisera, and, after Meroz has been cursed and Jael blessed, the Song ends by making an apparently derisive reference to the mother of Sisera waiting vainly for her son's victorious return. The contrast in theme and language between the introduction/conclusion and the rest of the Song of Deborah would indicate that the introduction and conclusion come from a time when the already existing Song was adapted in order to fit a cultic context. In other words, vv.12–30 of the Song belong to an early time, before the Song was brought into a cultic context, and so these verses are not to be interpreted against a cultic background. It is true that v.23 does refer to Yahweh, but this is only incidentally in the context of the curse to be pronounced on Meroz. In so far as Meroz is cursed for not coming 'to the help of the Lord', this would identify those who had participated as the people of Yahweh, but this does not in any way support the sort of cultic background to the Song which was described above. It was only at some later, indeterminable time and place that the Song of Deborah became a cultic hymn of praise to Yahweh,[18] but this later background does not help in the interpretation of vv.12–30.

If this is so far accurate, then the only possible interpretation of vv. 14–18 is that they refer to those tribes which had taken part in the battle against Sisera and to those which had stayed away. Coming immediately after v. 13, this list of tribes must be seen in the context of praise of those tribes which had 'marched down against the mighty' on behalf of Yahweh, and of reprimand for those tribes which had not fulfilled what the poet considered to be their duty in this respect. This view does not conflict with the first verse of this section, v. 12; it is quite unnecessary to see this as a summons to a victory celebration at which Deborah sings and Barak parades his victory trophies.[19] The verse may easily be understood to anticipate the victory of Barak over Sisera: just as Barak's task is to overcome the enemy and take captives, so Deborah also will have her part to play; this will be to inspire the warriors by her singing and chanting.[20]

With this view of the Song there does still exist, of course, the difficulty of the repeated reference to Zebulun and Naphtali in v. 18. However, this may be explained without recourse to the supposition that these were the only two tribes which fought against Sisera. Either this verse is a secondary addition to the Song, which was introduced in much the same way as the explicit reference to these tribes in the prose story of Judg. 4, or the verse is original and the intention is to emphasize these two tribes. This could be for one or both of two reasons: either the courageous part played by these tribes in the battle was particularly worthy of note, or the aim is to point up the contrast between these two tribes and those mentioned in the previous verses which had remained in the security of their own tribal territories. Indeed, it is hard to escape the conclusion that it is the intention of the poet here simply to make this contrast: just as later in the Song the curse on Meroz is immediately followed by the blessing on Jael,[21] so here the reprimand on Reuben, Gilead, Dan and Asher is immediately followed by praise for Zebulun and Naphtali. If this is the case, then it must be concluded that just as Zebulun and Naphtali are praised for their part in the battle, so Reuben, Gilead, Dan and Asher are reprimanded for staying away, and so also Ephraim, Benjamin, Machir, Zebulun and Issachar are mentioned for their participation in the battle, and not for their presence at a cultic festival.

This way of treating the Song of Deborah is not to be

contradicted by the assertion that participation in the battle would
have been obligatory, and so one would have expected a curse, like
that pronounced on Meroz, on those tribes which stayed away instead of a light reprimand. It is highly unlikely that any such obligation existed;[22] it can only be said that in the view of the poet it was
the duty of these tribes, as members of the people of Yahweh, to
take part in this battle. Nor can this view be contradicted by an
attempted classification of the Song of Deborah as a single type or
form of literature – it cannot be classed simply as a psalm, or a
victory song, or an epic poem, or a propaganda song, or a taunt
song. In fact, the Song of Deborah in its present form is a combination of all of these: it is a psalm according to the setting which
it eventually received and according to the introduction with
which it was supplied; it is a victory song in that it certainly does
celebrate the defeat of Sisera; it is an epic poem in that it does offer
a description of the battle and an account of the end of Sisera; it
also contains an element of propaganda in that, through praise
and reprimand, it aims to show the responsibility of the tribes as
the people of Yahweh; and, finally, it concludes with a taunt over
the mother of Sisera. In this way a variety of motifs have been
used in the composition of the Song; but to classify the Song
exclusively according to any one of them opens the way to a mis-
interpretation of the rest of the Song.

So, in answer to the first of the two questions which we earlier
directed to the Song, it may be said that the background of the
kernel of the Song of Deborah in vv. 12–30 and the situation out
of which it arose is the victory over Sisera. The tribes referred to
in vv. 14–18 are those which took part in and those which absented
themselves from the battle.[23] At a later stage the Song was taken
up into cultic use and was supplied with an introduction and conclusion in the style of the psalms.

The second of the two questions on the Song of Deborah is that
of the date of the event which it commemorates. This is an important matter from our point of view, for if it can be shown that
this successful combined operation of a number of Israelite tribes
took place at an early stage in the period of the judges, then there
is here good evidence for the existence of a federation, even if not
a federation of twelve tribes, which could act in unity relatively un-
hindered by the circumstances of settlement of the individual
tribes.

It is precisely at this point, however, that we stand on uncertain ground. A widespread view is that the battle took place *c.* 1125 BC. This is based on the argument that Judg. 5.19, which sites the battle 'at Taanach, by the waters of Megiddo', presupposes that Megiddo was itself unoccupied at this time; following on this, it has been held that archaeological evidence points to a gap in the occupation of Megiddo between 1150 BC and 1075 BC. However, this argument is weak both from the archaeological point of view, and from the point of view of the conclusion which has been drawn from Judg. 5.19. At precisely what point of time the gap in occupation of Megiddo is to be dated is far from generally agreed;[24] but quite apart from this, there is the even more serious objection that Judg. 5.19 does not imply what the exponents of this view propose. This verse can be taken to mean only exactly what it says: the battle took place at Taanach by the waters of Megiddo and not at Megiddo itself; there is nothing in these words either to imply or to preclude Megiddo's having been unoccupied at that time. So if the battle against Sisera is to be dated it will have to be by other means.

One approach towards the solution of the problem is to attempt a reconstruction of the chronology of the period in this part of Palestine up until the appearance of Sisera as the leader of a coalition of Canaanite kings. This involves especially the assignment of a relative dating to Shamgar and Sisera, and perhaps also Jabin, from which it might be possible to attain an absolute dating through correlating this with the time of the appearance of the Philistines in this area of northern Palestine.[25] According to this approach, Shamgar was a member of a Canaanite ruling family, opposed to the Philistines, who governed a large territory which must have extended into the plain of Megiddo. His Canaanite origin is to be concluded from his name and parentage given in Judg. 3.31,[26] while his status as a ruler may be concluded from the fact that he is mentioned in the Song of Deborah in Judg. 5.6. Shamgar must have begun that political development which resulted in the battle with Sisera.[27] Since Shamgar opposed the Philistines he must belong to the time that the Philistines appeared in this part of Palestine, and the latter events belongs to the time of the decline of Megiddo stratum VI in the second half of the twelfth century BC. However, in contrast to Shamgar, a Canaanite in power in this part of the land, and opposed to the Philistines, the Song of Deborah presents Sisera, a Philistine, at the head of a Canaanite coalition in this same area.[28] This signifies a great shift in power compared with the situation which existed under Shamgar. If Shamgar, a leading Canaanite opposed to the Philistines, belongs to the second half of the twelfth century BC, it is highly unlikely that a change, which resulted not only in a Canaanite–Philistine coalition against Israelite tribes but also in Philistine leadership of that coalition, could have taken place before the eleventh century BC. This, in turn, would suggest that this victory by Israelite tribes over a Canaanite–Philistine coalition led by Sisera should be seen in close connection with Israel's defeat by the Philistines at Aphek sometime in the course of the second half of the eleventh century BC.[29]

These particular arguments in favour of a late dating for the battle against Sisera are not really convincing. They depend heavily on a conjectured position and sphere of influence of Shamgar which cannot be demonstrated with any degree of certainty, and which, indeed, are rendered all the more problematical if, as we tried to show above, it is true that the verses of the Song of Deborah which refer to Shamgar belong to a secondary extension to the Song.[30] But even if the arguments which have been adduced in support of this date of the battle against Sisera are not very reliable, it is still probable that the conclusion is correct. By connecting the victory over Sisera with the defeat of Israel by the Philistines at Aphek, in the sense that the latter event followed soon after and was a consequence of the former event, it is possible to provide a context for both these battles. In part of I Sam. 4.1 we read: 'Now Israel went out to battle against the Philistines; they encamped at Ebenezer and the Philistines encamped at Aphek.' In the ensuing battle Israel was roundly defeated and put in subjection to the Philistines. However, the Old Testament record provides no context for this battle; nothing is said of the reason for this confrontation at this particular time and place. Since the Philistines had entered the land about a century earlier than this battle at Aphek, which took place towards the end of the eleventh century BC,[31] and since Aphek lay some distance north of the Philistine city-states, it is highly unlikely that the battle is to be explained simply on the basis of Philistine aims of expansion. If this were the background the battle would have been fought at an earlier time and probably also in that part of the land where, as the

Samson stories illustrate, border skirmishes between Israelites and Philistines did take place.

If this is the case, then it must be asked if the confrontation at Aphek has its background in Israelite aims of expansion, or at least in a situation in which Israelite tribes were felt to constitute a threat to the Philistines; such a situation would arise particularly if Israelite tribes made their presence felt in the plains of Palestine. It is the need to find such a situation in order to explain why Israel and the Philistines fought at Aphek which compels us to understand that the victory over Sisera was the prelude to the battle at Aphek. The occasion of the victory over Sisera is the only major advance of Israelite tribes into the plains of Palestine that we know of for this time, which could explain a battle between Israel and the Philistines at Aphek. Sisera may have been a Philistine, or at least related to them, and if so his defeat was the defeat of a Canaanite-Philistine coalition against Israel. But even if Sisera was not a Philistine, the victory of Israel would have been seen by the Philistines as a potential threat to their own position of power and superiority in the plains; therefore, the battle at Aphek must be seen as swift retaliation by the Philistines for the defeat of Sisera, in order that they might obviate any chance of Israel's gaining a position of permanent supremacy in this part of the plains of Palestine. Since it seems that Megiddo remained a Canaanite settlement after the defeat of Sisera,[32] there is all the more reason for looking for some such sequel as this to the Sisera episode. Thus, although this argument does not explain precisely why the battle with Sisera took place in this particular area and at this particular time, a difficulty which exists whatever date is assigned to the event, it is clear that by connecting the victory over Sisera with the defeat of Israel by the Philistines at Aphek in this way, it is possible to attain a good historical context for these events, a historical context which is at present lacking in the Old Testament tradition, but which is nevertheless demanded. To date the victory over Sisera at about 1125 BC, or at some earlier time, leaves it as an isolated event, and, in that it is then left without apparent consequences, it loses most of the momentous significance which it really had.

The victory over Sisera represents the first concerted incursion of Israelite tribes into the plains of Palestine from their primary settlement areas in the mountains. As such it signifies not just

Israelite expansion of territory, but the first attempt of a number of Israelite tribes acting together to incorporate fertile and profitable parts of the country into their own territory. It is unlikely, to say the least, that Israelite control of the plain of Esdraelon, gained through the defeat of Sisera, would have remained unchallenged for long, especially if, as seems to have been the case, the city of Megiddo was not occupied by Israel at the time. For this reason, then, it seems best to see the victory over Sisera in the general context of Israelite expansion into the plains of Palestine rather than as an isolated victory on the part of Israel without much cause or really appreciable effect. Israelite expansion into the plains, however, as a recognizable tendency on the part of Israelite tribes, belongs to a fairly advanced stage of their process of settlement; and, indeed, in so far as such a tendency would have provoked an immediate reaction on the part of the inhabitants of the plains, particularly the Philistines and other Sea Peoples, it seems that it was not until shortly before the rise of the monarchy that such attempts to expand into the plains were seriously undertaken. The battle between Israelite tribes and the Philistines at Aphek towards the end of the eleventh century BC also belongs in this context, and provides an eminently suitable sequel to Israel's first success represented by the victory over Sisera. The latter event should then be seen as the cause of a reaction which led to Philistine subjugation of Israel during the reign of Saul, and so also to a temporary halt in Israel's attempts to enlarge her territory. We would argue, therefore, that in the latter half of the eleventh century BC Israel defeated a coalition led by Sisera, and in turn was shortly afterwards met in battle and defeated by the Philistines at Aphek.[33]

The two conclusions we have reached on the Song of Deborah, first, that the tribes mentioned in it are those which took part and those which did not take part in the battle against Sisera, and, secondly, that the event commemorated in the Song is to be dated to the latter half of the eleventh century BC, are of some considerable importance for the whole question being investigated here. This is the first occasion in the period of the judges that we find a wide alliance of tribes taking part in a concerted action, and, moreover, an alliance which would have been wider if other tribes had fulfilled what the poet in the Song of Deborah claims to have been their duty. That this is so is scarcely simply a coincidence: it is unlikely that it is only because of our lack of information that we hear of no earlier concerted action of the tribes. There are two reasons for saying this: in the first place, probably one of the reasons for the composition of the Song of Deborah, and perhaps indeed the main reason, was that this occasion was unique in that such an alliance did appear; the Song does not only celebrate the victory, it celebrates also the appearance of the united tribes against a common enemy. In the second place, those traditions of wars in the period of the judges, which were investigated in the previous chapter, spoke of Israel acting in these wars; yet it was quite clear that they were in fact the action of a much more limited group of either one or two tribes. This is not the case with the battle against Sisera. It would seem justifiable, therefore, to argue that this was the first occasion of the appearance of such an alliance.

This being the case, a further observation may be made. The chief difference between those other battles and the one led by Barak against Sisera is that in the latter the northern tribes make their first appearance in common action with the mid-Palestinian tribes. Issachar, Zebulun and Naphtali fought in the battle, while Asher and Dan should have been there. In no other event did these northern tribes appear either alone or with the mid-Palestinian tribes. There was very good reason for this, for Judg. 1.27ff., in giving a list of those city-states which the tribes had been unable to conquer when they settled, shows that in fact there was a line of these foreign city-states from Dor on the coast, through Megiddo, Taanach and Ibleam to Bethshean situated near the Jordan,[34] a line which would have constituted an effective barrier between the Galilean and the mid-Palestinian tribes. It is this which prevented any earlier appearance of the Galilean tribes along with the others. However, the strength of this chain of city-states would have depended on the strength of the individual city-states of which it was composed, and since the city-state of Taanach was apparently destroyed towards the end of the twelfth century BC,[35] while the palace building and pottery objects found at Megiddo bear witness, in their poor standard, to a great decline in the strength of that city from the second half of the twelfth century BC on,[36] it is very likely that it was precisely with the aim of putting an end to the divisive influence of these city-states that there took place the battle against Sisera. But even if it cannot be

proved that this was the purpose of the battle, it may still be said
that the end of these city-states as a really effective dividing line
between the tribes provided the opportunity for the battle to take
place. For most of the period of the judges, therefore, the Galilean
tribes were separated by force of circumstances from contact with
the mid-Palestinian tribes. It was only towards the end of this
period, in the eleventh century BC, that common activity became
possible, and made its first appearance in the battle with Sisera.

Our examination of the Song of Deborah is not yet, however,
complete. The tribes referred to in the Song are: Ephraim, Benjamin, Machir, Zebulun, Issachar, Reuben, Gilead,[37] Dan, Asher
and Naphtali. Although only six of these tribes took part in the
battle, the other four, in the view of the poet, should also have been
there. All ten were expected to fight on Yahweh's behalf, all ten
therefore belong together as the people of Yahweh. The question
then must be raised: were those tribes, which are not mentioned
in the Song, but which we know later to have been Israelite, not
Israelite tribes at the time of the battle against Sisera? The tribes in
question are: Gad, Manasseh, Judah and Simeon. The tribe of
Levi is not mentioned either, but its absence could be accounted for
by the supposition that it was a priestly tribe, or a landless group
in the process of becoming a priestly tribe, at this time, and so
would not have been expected to fight in the battle alongside the
other tribes. But as for the other tribes to which no reference is
made, there are three possible explanations which must be considered: (1) the tribes may not have been formed by the time of
the war against Sisera; (2) the tribes may have existed at this time,
but were not yet reckoned as Israelite tribes; (3) the tribes may
have been Israelite tribes at this time, but may have been prevented
by force of circumstances from participating in the battle. Enough
has been said already on this subject as far as Manasseh and Gad
are concerned;[38] Manasseh probably did not yet exist as a tribe;
on the other hand, Gad, if it was in existence, was probably not
yet an Israelite tribe. So our main concern here is with the tribes
of Judah and Simeon. There is no reason to understand that Judah
and Simeon did not exist as tribes at the time of the battle against
Sisera. So, either they were not Israelite tribes or they were quite
unable to participate, a situation which was recognized by the
poet in the Song of Deborah. On the other hand, it is not enough
to say simply that the poet in the Song of Deborah did not intend

to give a full list of the tribes. This may not have been his primary
intention, but since he felt forced to censure some tribes for not
participating in the battle it must be assumed that the effect of his
tribal listing was that he named every Israelite tribe which, in his
view, could have been present.

It has been proposed[39] that the Song of Deborah presupposes
the existence of an amphictyony of ten members comprising those
tribes which are mentioned in the Song. If the existence of such
an amphictyony of ten members could be demonstrated, then
especially in view of a common, later use of the term 'Israel' with
reference to the northern kingdom it would be reasonable to
suppose that this amphictyony was called Israel, and that the
designation Israelite belonged to the members of this amphictyony, and that since Judah and Simeon are not mentioned in the
Song of Deborah they did not belong to the amphictyony and
therefore were not Israelite tribes. That such an amphictyony ever
existed is, however, extremely doubtful. Not only do many of the
arguments brought forward earlier, particularly in connection
with the existence of a central sanctuary, apply also here, but it has
also been noted that the battle against Sisera was probably the
first occasion of common action on the part of the mid-Palestinian
and the Galilean tribes, which until this time had been separated
by unconquered Canaanite city-states. The Song of Deborah can,
therefore, provide no support for the theory of an amphictyony
of ten tribes.

If this is the case, the only other way to define an Israelite tribe
in this early period, at least as far as the Song of Deborah is concerned, is to use that description which the Song itself applies to
those who took part in the battle: they were the people of Yahweh
(Judg. 5.13, 23), they were tribes which acknowledged Yahweh as
their God and who saw the battle against Sisera as a battle waged
on behalf of Yahweh.[40] On this basis, however, there is certainly
no reason for taking Judah and Simeon as non-Israelite tribes.
Judah and Simeon in the period of the judges were as much the
people of Yahweh as were the other tribes mentioned in the Song.
There is no evidence for the view that the worship of Yahweh
was introduced into Judah[41] only in the time of David, and indeed
such evidence as we do possess would suggest rather that the rise
of the monarchy presupposes the existence of that entity called the
people of Yahweh embracing both Judah and the northern

tribes.[42] This means that there can be only one answer to the
problem of the absence of reference to Judah and Simeon in the
Song of Deborah. The reason must be that it was recognized that
it was quite impossible for Judah and Simeon to participate in the
battle against Sisera.[43] There must have existed historical conditions which prevented these southern tribes joining the northern
tribes, and these circumstances were recognized and appreciated
by the poet in the Song of Deborah. There was, therefore, no
occasion for any relevant reference to Judah and Simeon in this
particular context.

That we are correct in thinking that the historical and geographical conditions of the time separated Judah from the remaining tribes in the north[44] is supported by two considerations. In the
first place, the settlement of the tribes which went to make up
Judah took place apparently directly from the south. The Judean
tribes did not enter the land by crossing the Jordan from the east
along with one or more of the other tribes. Rather, they migrated
into the hill country south of Jerusalem directly from the south,
and settled independently of the movements of the other tribes.[45]
Apart from general indications, such as are to be found in Judg.
1.1ff., 16ff. that this is what happened, the specific traditions which
provide the main help here are those which deal with Caleb's conquest of Hebron.[46] These traditions, to be found in Deut. 1.22ff.;
Josh. 14.6ff.; 15.13ff.; Judg. 1.20, which, since they presuppose
Caleb's possession of Hebron and seek to explain this circumstance,
have an aetiological character, undoubtedly have good historical
tradition behind them. This must be so not only because the
tradition would not otherwise have ascribed such an important
conquest to Caleb, but also because there is, in Num. 13–14, a
tradition which in its original form probably told of the settlement
of Hebron by Caleb coming directly from the south. In its present
form this tradition tells of an abortive attempt at invasion of the
land from the south, abortive because Israel had disobeyed the
instructions of Yahweh. This disobedience was the result of a discouraging report on conditions in the land brought back by the
spies whom the people had sent there. Two of these spies, however, Joshua and Caleb, had not brought back a discouraging
report, and for their faithfulness they were promised that they
would go in and possess the land while the rest of their generation
would die in the wilderness. The clear purpose of the JE narrative

in these chapters is, as with the other Caleb traditions, to explain how Caleb[47] came to possess the district of Hebron. On the other hand, this narrative has apparently taken up and transformed a tradition of an actual settlement of Hebron by Caleb coming directly from the south. This seems more credible than the idea that Caleb, after wandering with the rest of his generation in the wilderness until that generation had died, accompanied Joshua in his invasion from the east and thence proceeded south to Hebron. The reason for the present Old Testament presentation of the course of events is simply the desire to obviate the chance of giving rise to the impression that the conquest was anything other than a united assault of all Israel under Joshua coming from the east.

The second point to be considered here is that the Old Testament tradition offers good enough reason for Judah's enforced isolation from the rest of the tribes in the north after it had settled independently of those tribes. As well as giving a list of Canaanite city-states which isolated the Galilean tribes from the mid-Palestinian tribes, Judg. 1 also refers to other cities in the southern part of the land which remained unconquered. So Judg. 1.34ff. mention Har-heres, Aijalon and Shaalbim[48] as unconquered cities which remained in the hands of the 'Amorites'.[49] Furthermore, it is known from elsewhere that both Gezer and Jerusalem remained in foreign hands until the time of the monarchy.[50] Thus, there existed between Judah and its northern neighbours an unconquered belt of land still controlled by the Canaanites. This would effectively have prevented Judah's sending a contingent to take part in the battle against Sisera.[51] It is probably this situation which was recognized by the poet in the Song of Deborah who could, then, attach neither praise nor blame to the southern tribes in this connection.

In view of this, moreover, it is not surprising that Judah and Simeon do not generally appear acting along with the other tribes in the period of the judges. The one possible exception to this is to be found in the traditions dealing with Samson,[52] for here, in Judg. 15.9ff., Judah does appear in contact with the tribe of Dan. If this is original to this tradition, it does, however, constitute the exception that proves the rule that Judah was isolated from the northern tribes. The Samson traditions presuppose Dan's living in its first place of settlement to the west of Jerusalem on

the border of Philistine territory. The tribe of Dan would then
have formed a bridge between Judah and the north, the only contact which Judah would have had with the other tribes. As soon,
however, as Dan was forced by pressure from the Philistines to
give up this place of settlement – and this must have happened at a
fairly early stage[53] – and migrate to a new area far to the north,
even this slight contact between Judah and the other tribes would
have been broken. Judah would thus have ended up as much cut
off from the mid-Palestinian tribes as were also the Galilean tribes
because of the chain of foreign city-states which straddled the
northern part of the land.

However, just as the dividing influence of the northern Canaanite city-states was finally broken so that the Galilean and mid-
Palestinian tribes could come together, so also the power of those
city-states which separated Judah from the mid-Palestinian tribes
must eventually have been destroyed. We have already seen that
Judah formed part of the kingdom of Saul at some stage of his
reign,[54] so it must have been at the latest during the monarchy of
Saul that Judah's isolation from the north came to an end. When
this happened precisely is not an easy question to answer, but
there are some indications that it was in fact as a result of Saul's
early military successes.

In the first place, there is no indication, for the period before
Saul, of any Israelite victory in this area which could have led to
the decline of the power of the southern city-states. In the second
place, it is not the simple existence of these city-states as foreign
holdings which would have isolated Judah from the north; Gezer
and Jerusalem were foreign enclaves until after the time of Saul,
but they did not prevent Saul's movements through Judean territory. It is the military power of these city-states and the support
they would have received from other non-Israelites that would
have made this division between the tribes.

One thing which emerged from our earlier study of the battle
against Sisera was that Israel's victory over Sisera was seen by the
Philistines as a threat to their own supremacy in the plains of
Palestine. To this extent, the continued power of the Canaanites
would have been in the interests of the Philistines as a desirable
check on Israelite growth and expansion. If this is the case, then
the Philistines would presumably have supported the Canaanites
against the Israelites, and so the end of the power of the Canaanite

city-states would have required the defeat of the Philistines also. It is precisely such a victory over the Philistines in this area which is ascribed by the tradition to the early part of Saul's reign. The Philistines had established garrisons in the hill-country of Ephraim and Benjamin whence they were driven by Israel and, according to I Sam. 14.31, were struck down 'from Michmash to Aijalon'.[55] This victory would have marked the end of Canaanite-Philistine obstruction between Judah and the north, and the way would then have been left open for Saul to include also Judah within his kingdom.[56] Only as a result of this, then, could Judah take an active part in common enterprises with the other tribes.

It is improbable that the reign of Saul should be seen as the time of origin of that Israel, the people of Yahweh, which is addressed by the prophets and which is the subject of the Pentateuchal tradition. In this sense, the unity of Israel under Saul presupposes an earlier unity of the tribes; they were related in that they all acknowledged Yahweh as their God, quite apart from any common historical background they may have had in the time before they settled in the land. However, an active unity of the tribes after settlement does not appear until the time of Saul; it is only from this time on that such unity as the tribes did have found active, concrete expression. This unity of the tribes under Saul certainly cannot be explained simply by reference to the threat posed by the Philistines,[57] nor simply as a result of Saul's military victories; but it does appear, nevertheless, that because of the circumstances of settlement of the Israelite tribes and their inability at first to overcome those forces which divided them, a common political or cultic life was impossible until the rise of Saul.

The main object of this book has been to demonstrate that the evidence in favour of the existence of an amphictyony in ancient Israel is slight indeed. Furthermore, the evidence against the existence of such a league compels us to admit that the traditions dealing with this period, when their schematic framework is disregarded, are historically reliable in the impression which they give of the practical disunity of the Israelite tribes before the appearance of Saul. There is no evidence of the existence of a common, central sanctuary to which these tribes, or their representatives, repaired at regular intervals to participate in common worship. Instead, there was a multiplicity of sanctuaries, and no one of them can be said to have surpassed the others in claiming a particular allegiance from all the tribes. It may be that the deposit of the ark at a certain sanctuary exalted that sanctuary above the others for the duration of its possession of the ark, and for this reason that sanctuary may have formed the object of pilgrimage, perhaps even from outside the territory of the tribe in which it lay. But it is a far cry from this to the view that the sanctuary in possession of the ark was the central sanctuary of an amphictyony, at which regular festivals were celebrated, and for the maintenance of which the members of the amphictyony were responsible. It is much preferable to believe that the sanctuaries of which we read in the Old Testament had their own fame and their own circles of worshippers within the tribal areas in which they lay, So, for the service of the Galilean tribes there was the sanctuary on Mount Tabor which lay on the border of Zebulun, Naphtali and Issachar; for the mid-Palestinian tribes there were sanctuaries at Shechem, Gilgal, Bethel, Shiloh and perhaps also Mizpah; and for Judah there was the famous sanctuary of Mamre by the Calebite city Hebron, which had particular associations with Abraham.[58] Probably also the Transjordanian tribes had their own sanctuaries.[59] Not only does this fit in with the division of the tribes in west Jordan into three groups separated by foreign city-states, but the fact that a number of sanctuaries can be shown for the mid-Palestinian tribes corresponds to the fact that it is with this group that the Old Testament tradition for the period of the judges is mainly concerned.

While there is, therefore, no evidence of common cultic activity of all the tribes at a central sanctuary, there is no evidence either of common political activity. Although the traditions dealing with war in the period of the judges now stand in a framework which tells of the oppression of Israel and the deliverance of Israel, it is clear that these traditions referred originally only to a limited group and that it was at a secondary stage of their history that they were brought into the context of all Israel. However, it is within this sphere of political activity that it is possible to trace some steps in the development by which the Israelite tribes progressed from acting as individual units to the stage of taking the field together in time of battle. The first step in this development was the battle against Sisera. Here, for the first time, the Galilean tribes appear alongside the mid-Palestinian tribes. The second step was somewhat later; this was the expulsion of the Philistines from the southern mountain area by Saul, which opened the way for real contact between Judah and its northern neighbours.

Thus, the object of removing the barriers which separated the tribes was not totally achieved until the time of Saul; and indeed the first step towards achieving this aim had not been taken until shortly before this in the battle against Sisera in the second half of the eleventh century BC. However, in the earlier discussion of the tribal lists it was concluded that neither of the two basic types of tribal list can be derived from, or can be based on a prototype which derives from, a time earlier than the battle against Sisera.[60] This means that if these tribal lists reflect historical conditions, that is, if they are based, not on a theoretical idea of Israel, but on an actual Israel consisting of precisely these tribes, and if, moreover, they are to be claimed as reflections of conditions before the rise of the monarchy, then the Israel which is reflected here was the Israel which existed in the short period, of about fifty years, between the battle against Sisera and the rise of Saul. This may be so, but if it is then all there is in these tribal lists is a series, or, rather, two series, of tribes reckoned to be Israelite. There is no question of these tribal lists reflecting the existence of an amphictyony consisting of the twelve tribes named. Not only was the barrier between Judah and the north not removed until the time of Saul, but also during most of these years the whole land was in complete subjection to the Philistines as a result of Israel's defeat at the battle at Aphek.

It may, therefore, be concluded that the existence of an amphictyony in ancient Israel is a theory which is supported neither by the most important and basic evidence which has been brought forward, that of the tribal lists and the evidence for the existence of a central sanctuary, nor by the less important evidence, that for the existence of an office of judge of Israel, one of the functions of which is supposed to have been the fixing of the tribal boundaries. Furthermore, it is only through observing the Israelite tribes in war that it is possible to trace the steps by which they came to the full expression of their unity under their first king Saul.[61]

IV

CONCLUSION

We have come to the end of our treatment of Israel in the period of the judges. However, the subject cannot simply be left at this point. At the beginning of this study the investigation of the possibility of the existence of an amphictyony in ancient Israel was put within the context of a search for the origin of that entity we know as Israel, an entity which, in spite of its outward political divisions, is the one people of Yahweh. It was also indicated then that this united people of Yahweh is unlikely to have originated in the time of the monarchy. The monarchy, rather, presupposes the existence of this Israel. In broad terms the main problem emerged as one of finding historical conditions from which it might be possible to explain the fact that Yahweh was acknowledged as God by both Judah and the northern tribes, so that Judah and the northern tribes together constituted the people of Yahweh. As a result of our treatment of the period of the judges it is clear that this period cannot be considered to present the historical conditions for which we are looking. Not only is it impossible to think in terms of an amphictyony for this period, but also Judah was physically isolated from the northern tribes until the advent of the monarchy under Saul. Consequently, two courses remain open: on the one hand, Judah may have been a non-Israelite tribe which accepted the worship of Yahweh only in the time of Saul or David; on the other hand, the historical conditions which will explain the fact of the worship of Yahweh being common to Judah and the northern tribes must lie in the time before the settlement of the Israelite tribes.

As we have already seen, the first option must be dismissed. The traditions of the Exodus deliverance and the Sinai covenant formed an integral part of worship in both Judah and Jerusalem in the period of the monarchy,[1] and it is unlikely that they are to be considered merely as transplantations thither in the time of Saul or David of what were originally specifically northern traditions. It is true that, since Jerusalem was a Jebusite city until its capture by David, it was only in the time of David that Israelite cultic tradition gained entry into Jerusalem;[2] on the other hand, however, it cannot be maintained that this tradition brought to Jerusalem in the time of David was originally purely north Israelite tradition.[3] There are two points which support this statement. First of all, Jerusalem had to be made acceptable from a cultic point of view to the south as well as to the north. If, as seems to be the case, it is true that the reason for David's choice of Jerusalem as his capital was that this was a neutral city from which, without charge of favouritism, he could effectively govern both parts of his kingdom,[4] it is unlikely that he would have permitted this neutrality to be prejudiced by allowing peculiarly northern cultic traditions into the worship in his capital. In other words, the Yahwistic tradition which is found in the Jerusalem temple must have been as much the heritage of Judah as it was the heritage of the northern tribes.

There is, however, a second point which can support the argument that Judah, while being completely independent of the northern tribes in the period of the judges, shared in a common faith in Yahweh with those northern tribes in that period. What is more, it is through a consideration of this second point that it will be possible to bring to light those historical conditions in which the unity of Israel as the people of Yahweh was founded.

We must refer here once more to those traditions dealing with Caleb's settlement of Hebron. For not only does Num. 13–14 preserve a tradition which told originally of a movement of Calebites directly northwards into the region of Hebron, but Caleb is also treated by this tradition as a worshipper of Yahweh. That the tradition is authentic in both these respects is hardly to be doubted.[5] Unless there was a very strong tradition that the Calebites did settle this region and did, moreover, come into this region as worshippers of Yahweh, it is most unlikely that the name of Caleb would have been preserved as such. This conclusion can only be supported by the fact that Caleb does not appear as an Israelite tribe in any of the tribal lists.

Furthermore, the starting point of this movement northwards

by Calebites is said in Num. 13–14 to have been Kadesh. That this is an original feature of the tradition cannot, of course, be proved; however, in view of the fact that the movement was directly from the south northwards, and also of the fact that the Calebites were worshippers of Yahweh, it seems likely that they had at least been in contact with Kadesh even if they did not migrate to Hebron directly from there.[6] Kadesh occupies a significant place in the traditions of Israel's pre-settlement days; it is, in fact, the focal point of the traditions of Israel's wilderness wandering. While the relationship between Kadesh and Sinai, in both the literature and the history of tribal movements in the area, is a too complex question to be embarked on here, Kadesh was, nevertheless, an important centre of wandering groups of tribes or clans which worshipped Yahweh.[7] It is from here that the Calebites, as followers of Yahweh, probably ultimately derive, and it was from here that they migrated eventually to settle in the region of Hebron and so introduced Yahwism to this area. Under these conditions it is clear how Judah, in the period of the judges, could have been totally separated from the northern tribes and yet could have shared in a common faith with these tribes.

However, this is not all that can be said. Yahwism came into the area of Judah directly from Kadesh as a result of the migration of Caleb to Hebron;[8] but there is just as strong a direct connection of the mid-Palestinian tribes with Kadesh. Yahweh was worshipped at Shechem in the form of a covenant ceremony,[9] and since our discussion has already shown that the mid-Palestinian tribes were separated from the other tribes to the north and the south for most of the period of the judges, it must be concluded that Yahwism came to this area independently of its appearance in Judah.[10] In other words, some part of the later mid-Palestinian group of tribes was also at Kadesh whence it wandered again eventually to appear in the region of Shechem. This is quite in line with the Old Testament tradition of a wandering from the region of Kadesh into the southern part of Transjordan and then northwards, so that west Jordan was entered from the east opposite Jericho.[11] Thus, one must reckon with a number of movements into the land, stemming ultimately from the region of Kadesh. There was at least one movement, that led by Caleb, which went directly north to settle in the southern part of the land, while another went round the borders of the land to enter west Jordan finally from the east. The chronological relationship of these movements cannot be established with any certainty,[12] but it may at least be established that they derived from Kadesh in which district the various clans and tribes involved had come to acknowledge Yahweh as their God.

If this is the case, then it must be to Kadesh that we should look for the origin of that unity of Israel as the people of Yahweh, which existed quite independently of the political structures which brought division, especially between north and south. It was at Kadesh that the Israel addressed by the prophets was founded. This is not to say that the ancestors of all the later tribes of Israel were at Kadesh; but what it does mean is simply that the people of Yahweh came into existence at Kadesh; here it divided and entered the land by various routes. As a consequence of the circumstances of settlement of these separate elements of the people of Yahweh, contact between them was impossible. This is the situation which is reflected in the Book of Judges apart from its deuteronomistic framework. The traditions here tell of local events which involved the individual tribes and which were related primarily in the context of the individual tribes. Only at a secondary stage of their development have these traditions been set in a rather artificial chronological order and recounted as the traditions of all Israel. This was a natural development; for each of those tribes, or each small group of tribes, though separated by force of circumstances from the others, was still a part of Israel the people of Yahweh, and in so far as it was such a part its experiences were the experiences of the people.

The divisions between the tribes were not finally removed until the time of Saul, when the barriers dividing Judah from the north were demolished. During this time also it must be understood that the worship of Yahweh spread; by Caleb it had been brought to Hebron, and by some part of the mid-Palestinian tribes it had been brought to Shechem, and from these two centres it radiated to embrace both northern and southern tribes. At some time, which must have been after the battle against Sisera, the now extended people of Yahweh was defined in clearer terms, in the form of the descendants of twelve brothers, the sons of the patriarch Jacob. This is a reflection, not of an amphictyonic organization of twelve tribes, but of a community all of whose members acknowledged Yahweh as their God, and whose unity had been founded at Kadesh.

NOTES

INTRODUCTION

1. See particularly Danell, *Studies in the Name Israel in the Old Testament*; and, for a study of an individual prophetic book, Beyerlin, *Die Kulttraditionen Israels in der Verkündigung des Propheten Micha*.

2. Cf. e.g., I Kings 12.20; 15.33; 16.8 etc.; Amos 3.14; 5.4; Hos. 5.1ff.; Jer. 3.12ff. etc.

3. Cf. Micah 3.1, 8, 9; 6.2, and Beyerlin, *Kulttraditionen Israels*, pp. 16, 24; Jer. 2.4, 14, 31, and Danell, *Studies in the Name Israel*, pp. 209ff.

4. Cf. e.g., Micah 5.1 (EVV v. 2); Jer. 5.15 (cf. v. 11); 31.33 (cf. vv. 27, 31). For the period before 721 BC the ground is less certain. However, it is likely that both Amos and Hosea knew the word Israel as a designation of the whole people of Yahweh. For Amos this judgment is not wholly dependent on the authenticity of 9.11ff. (cf. v. 14), since 3.1 is unlikely to have only the northern kingdom in mind. For Hosea, cf. 9.10.

5. We are not concerned here, therefore, with the origin of Yahwism as such. On the theory of the Kenite origin of the worship of Yahweh, cf. Budde, *The Religion of Israel to the Exile*, pp. 18ff.; Schmökel, *JBL* 52, 1933, pp. 212ff.; Rowley, *From Joseph to Joshua*, pp. 149ff.; Newman, *The People of the Covenant*, pp. 25f., 83ff., 138f. This theory is rejected by Kaufmann, *The Religion of Israel from its Beginnings to the Babylonian Exile*, pp. 242ff.; Volz, *Mose und sein Werk*, p. 59; Brekelmans, *OTS* 10, 1954, pp. 215ff. (for further bibliography on the subject, cf. Weippert, *The Settlement of the Israelite Tribes in Palestine*, pp. 105f., n. 14). Our present concern is with the origin of Yahwism only in so far as it will elucidate the origin of the national religious consciousness of that people which came to be called Israel.

6. It has been conjectured by Noth, *Das System der zwölf Stämme Israels*, pp. 91ff. (cf. also Newman, *The People of the Covenant*, pp. 78ff.), that the name was first used of an early association of the six Leah tribes centred round Shechem before the settlement of the mid-Palestinian tribes. The earliest occurrence of the name is in line 27 of the Stele of Merneptah: 'Israel is laid waste, his seed is not.' But it is impossible to determine to whom reference is made here. It has been held by Wilson, in *ANET*, p. 378, n. 18 (for others holding the same view, see the references in Rowley, *From Joseph to Joshua*, p. 30, n. 2), that, since the name is written with the determinative of the people and not of the land as otherwise in the stele, the reference is to the 'children of Israel in or near Palestine, but not yet as a settled people'; thus, the stele is

said to be important for the date of the conquest. However, since the chronology of Israel's early period is still far from certain, and since the origin of the name Israel is obscure and the time of its adoption by the tribes uncertain, it would be hazardous to base any conclusions on the reference, cf. Noth, *History of Pentateuchal Traditions*, p. 258, n. 655; *idem, The History of Israel*, p. 3; cf. also Eissfeldt, in *CAH* II ch. xxvi (a), p. 14. On the meaning of the name Israel, cf. Coote, *HTR* 65, 1972, pp. 137ff.

7. On this, cf. especially Alt, *Essays on Old Testament History and Religion*, pp. 173ff., 241ff. See further Smend, in *Fourth World Congress of Jewish Studies* 1, pp. 58ff. Alt's view of the Davidic monarchy as founded on the personal union (in David) of the northern and southern tribes, has been stringently criticized by Buccellati, *Cities and Nations of Ancient Syria*, pp. 148ff. There are two points to be made here, however: (*a*) even if David's empire was a single, united empire, it was marked by the increasing estrangement of the northern tribes from the southern tribes (cf. Buccellati, *Cities and Nations of Ancient Syria*, pp. 148ff.); (*b*) the statement of the elders of the northern tribes to the Judean David 'we are your bone and your flesh' (II Sam. 5.1) presupposes the existence of this unity of Israel before the time of David.

8. The term Canaanite is difficult to define, and it is doubtful to what extent one can speak of an ethnic difference between Canaanite and Israelite. Probably, indeed, Canaanite elements did contribute towards the formation of some of the Israelite tribes which eventually formed the state, but the extent to which this took place is largely a matter for conjecture; cf. Newman, *The People of the Covenant*, p. 110, n. 21, who suggests that the 'concubine' tribes of Gad, Asher, Dan and Naphtali were largely Canaanite. Apart from differences in religion, the distinction between Israelite and Canaanite is not so much ethnic as cultural: it lies in Israelite opposition to the Canaanite city-state culture, cf. Noth, *The Laws in the Pentateuch*, p. 29, n. 64.

9. Cf. Herrmann, *TLZ* 87, 1962, col. 570; Alt, *Essays*, p. 191, n. 47, p. 216 and n. 111; Mowinckel, in *Von Ugarit nach Qumran*, pp. 137f.

10. Cf. especially Schunck, *Benjamin*, pp. 124ff.; Eissfeldt, in *CAH* II ch. xxxiv, pp. 39f.

11. I Sam. 15.12. The historicity of this narrative has been disputed; cf. Soggin, *Das Königtum in Israel*, pp. 55ff., with references. However, the present argument does not depend solely on this point.

12. I Sam. 22.3ff.

13. I Sam. 27.1.

14. Cf. I Sam. 13.1. The Hebrew expression used here for 'two years' is unique (cf. Driver, *Notes on the Hebrew Text of the Books of Samuel*, p. 97), and it is sometimes argued that this notice is wrong (cf. Eissfeldt, in *CAH* II ch. xxxiv, p. 39), and that on historical grounds twelve or twenty years should be taken as the length of Saul's reign. However, whatever is substituted on textual grounds there is no adequate historical reason for carrying out any change, cf. Noth, *Überlieferungsgeschichtliche Studien*, pp. 24f.; *idem, History of Israel*, pp. 176f.

15. Cf. Noth, *History of Pentateuchal Traditions*, pp. 42ff.

16. Cf. Noth, *System*.

17. On the deuteronomistic history the basic work is again by Noth, cf.

his *Überlieferungsgeschichtliche Studien*. See also Gray, *Joshua, Judges and Ruth*, pp. 1ff. For a critical evaluation of Noth's view, cf. Eissfeldt, *Introduction*, pp. 242ff.; and, in some disagreement with Noth, cf. Weiser, *Introduction*, pp. 146, 180ff.; Fohrer, *Introduction*, pp. 192ff.

18. Such a process is in fact hinted at even within the deuteronomistic presentation in that it places the story of the migration of the tribe of Dan (Judg. 17–18), which is a settlement story, at a late stage in the period of the judges.

Chapter I

1. On this, cf. Noth, *History of Israel*, pp. 1ff., 53ff., 68ff.
2. Cf. also Horwitz, *CBQ* 35, 1973, pp. 69f.
3. Cf. Noth, *System*, pp. 43ff.
4. The short notice on the birth of Dinah in Gen. 30.21 is not original in this list. This is clear from the fact that it contains no etymology of the name while the rest of the names are supplied with etymologies, cf. Noth, *System*, p. 9.
5. Cf. Noth, *System*, pp. 11ff.
6. Noth, *System*, pp. 14ff.
7. Noth, *System*, pp. 20ff.
8. Noth, *System*, p. 24.
9. Noth does not commit himself on the question of whether or not there is any actual historical connection between the old 'secular' tribe of Levi and the priestly tribe, cf. *System*, p. 25, n. 3; *History of Israel*, p. 88, n. 2 (on the point see also Weippert, *The Settlement of the Israelite Tribes in Palestine*, p. 43, n. 139). Why it was that Gad in particular was 'promoted' to the third place in the system of Num. 26 is not so clear. One could perhaps argue that it had a historical background in the absorption of Reuben by Gad, cf. Zobel, *Stammesspruch und Geschichte*, pp. 64f., and see also the Moabite Stone, line 10, where Gad is taken to lie on Moab's northern border and not Reuben as would be expected. The name of the tribe of Reuben would then have been preserved simply to maintain the number twelve of the tribes. But if this is the case, it removes the basis from the explanation for the omission of Levi in the first place.
10. Cf. Noth, *System*, pp. 126ff.
11. On this, cf. Alt, *Essays*, pp. 135ff.
12. Cf. Noth, *System*, pp. 7f., 30.
13. Cf. Noth, *System*, pp. 46ff. For a short description of the Greek amphictyony with some bibliography, cf. Buccellati, *Cities and Nations of Ancient Syria*, p. 114; de Vaux, *HTR* 64, 1971, pp. 417ff.
14. Just as the number twelve had a practical significance based on the number of months in the year, so the basis of the federation of the *triginta populi Latini* would have been the number of days in the month, cf. Noth, *System*, pp. 52f.
15. Noth, *System*, p. 48.
16. This is the case especially with the sanctuary of Apollo at Delphi.

17. For an illuminating instance of the disunity of the amphictyony, reference may be made to the time of the Persian war under Xerxes. On this occasion many Greek states were passively, and some (e.g. Thessaly) actively, pro-Persia, while Xerxes at one time thought that he could persuade the Athenians over to his side, cf. Herodotus VII 130ff.

18. Cf. Noth, *System*, p.57; de Vaux, *HTR* 64, 1971, p.418.

19. Cf. Noth, *System*, pp.63f.

20. This conclusion is based on the observation that the Leah tribes were a fixed group of six tribes, cf. above and *System*, pp.75ff., 92ff.

21. *System*, pp.65ff.

22. *System*, pp.72f.

23. *System*, p.86. With the earlier six tribe (Leah) amphictyony, each member would have had the charge of the sanctuary for two months in the year.

24. *System*, p.96.

25. Noth, *System*, pp.93ff., connects this formula specifically with the ark, and thus accounts for its later use in the Jerusalem sanctuary where the ark was deposited by Solomon.

26. *System*, pp.89f.

27. In Israel the tribal representative was the *nāśi'*, corresponding to the Greek ἱερομνήμων; a list of the twelve Israelite *nᵉśi'im* is to be found in Num.1.5–15; cf. *System*, p.97.

28. Noth, *System*, p.98, thinks specifically of the religious and moral prohibitions of the form of Ex.22.27 (EVV v.28).

29. Cf. *System*, pp.100ff.; von Rad, *Old Testament Theology* 1, p.264. The crime committed by the men of Gibeah is called '*nᵉbālāh* (folly) in Israel', which Noth takes as an example of the idiomatic speech of the amphictyony designating a violation of the unwritten, customary law.

Chapter II

1. Cf. Irwin, *RB* 72, 1965, pp.161ff.

2. Cf. Smend, *Yahweh War and Tribal Confederation*, p.16.

3. Cf. Buccellati, *Cities and Nations of Ancient Syria*, p.114; de Vaux, *HTR* 64, 1971, p.424.

4. For a short review of some main objections to the theory, cf. Smend, *EvT* 31, 1971, pp.623ff.

5. Cf. Noth, *System*, pp.15f.

6. Cf. Noth, *System*, p.16, n.2.

7. Cf. Noth, *System*, pp.19f.

8. *System*, p.15, n.1, pp.16ff.

9. *System*, pp.23f.

10. The pre-eminence of Ephraim in the period of the judges is reflected, for example, in Judg.8.1ff.; 12.1ff.

11. Cf. Hoftijzer, *NedTTs* 14, 1959–60, pp.256f. See also further below, and Lehming, *VT* 13, 1963, pp.74ff.

12. Gen.37.3, in which Joseph is described as the son of Jacob's old age, apparently understands Joseph to be the youngest of the brothers. Yet the

dreams of Joseph presuppose the existence of eleven brothers of Joseph, and elsewhere Benjamin is the younger son of Rachel.

13. This presupposes Noth's view that J and E, because of their similarities, go back to a common basis (G), cf. *History of Pentateuchal Traditions,* pp. 38ff. If, however, Noth's view is rejected, and one were to follow Mowinckel, *Tetrateuch-Pentateuch-Hexateuch,* pp. 6ff., in seeing E not as an independent Pentateuchal document, but as the result of the incorporation into the written J of those differences which resulted from the further oral transmission of the tradition which had earlier been committed to writing in J, then it would be possible to argue that the order of the sons of Joseph given in Gen. 48 and elsewhere is a literary presentation which originated in the time of the composition of J, probably during the reign of Solomon. Because of the very fragmentary nature of the so-called document E, Mowinckel's hypothesis is attractive, and in any case is certainly not to be seen as impossible; for a view similar to that of Mowinckel, cf. Albright, *Yahweh and the Gods of Canaan,* pp. 25ff.

14. For this, cf. Hoftijzer, *NedTTs* 14, 1959–60, pp. 259f.

15. Cf. above p. 112, n. 9.

16. In the numbers which it has assigned to the tribe of Manasseh, Num. 26.34 shows that it has taken the place as first-born, which Gen. 48 assigned to Manasseh simply in order to emphasize the ultimate greatness of Ephraim, as literally true. Even if Noth is right in saying that the numbers in this list are a secondary feature of it (cf. *System,* pp. 130f.), it is probably the case that this understanding dictated the order of the sons of Joseph given in the list itself. On the basis of the numbers given in the lists Mendenhall, *JBL* 77, 1958, p. 63, argues that Num. 1 is earlier than Num. 26.

17. It is assumed that Benjamin was originally part of this list, but was later omitted because of the separate Benjamin tradition in Gen. 35.16–20.

18. The unique order which appears here cannot be explained with any certainty. For a suggestion, cf. Noth, *System,* p. 13, n. 2.

19. I Chron. 2.1f. is an exception to this, for here, although Gad and Asher are found together, Dan is separated from Naphtali by Joseph and Benjamin. Whether this is to be seen as simply a scribal error or as based on reasoning unknown to us is not clear, cf. also Noth, *System,* p. 13, n. 1.

20. Cf. Noth, *System,* pp. 8f.

21. Cf. Lehming, *VT* 13, 1963, pp. 74ff.

22. Cf. above p. 19.

23. The question must, therefore, be raised at this point as to the possibility that just as Gen. 37.3 apparently ignores the existence of Benjamin, so also the narrative in Gen. 29–30 never had an account of the birth of Benjamin. This possibility cannot be ruled out, though it is not possible to arrive at a certain decision.

24. Cf. above pp. 9f.

25. In the same way Gen. 49.3f. presupposes the present weakness of Reuben, and explains this by reference to an event in the past in which Reuben played an ignominious role. In the case of Reuben, the event is recorded in Gen. 35.22.

26. Even this cannot be taken as absolutely certain, however. It is worth

noting that in Ex. 32.26ff. Levi is praised for its fierceness, and is considered to have consecrated itself to Yahweh by slaying covenant-breaking fellow Israelites.

27. Cf. e.g., Josh. 13.14; 18.7.

28. Cf. Zobel, *Stammesspruch und Geschichte*, pp. 65ff., 70ff.; Gunneweg, *Leviten und Priester*, pp. 44ff.; Hoftijzer, *NedTTs* 14, 1959–60, p. 258, n. 3. De Vaux, *Ancient Israel*, p. 368, thinks that Gen. 49.5–7 refers to the non-priestly tribe of Levi because 'we know that Levi formed part of the old system of the Twelve Tribes'. This, however, seems to be a rather circular argument since it is precisely Gen. 49.5–7 which is used to prove that Levi was a member of a system of twelve tribes.

29. On this, cf. Cody, *A History of Old Testament Priesthood*, pp. 58ff.; Abba, in *IDB* 3, p. 888a.

30. On this term, cf. Cody, *Old Testament Priesthood*, pp. 54ff.

31. The possibility has been raised that Simeon and Levi are not original to the tradition of Gen. 34, but that their presence there is dependent on their association in Gen. 49.5–7. However, on this, cf. Cody, *Old Testament Priesthood*, p. 36, n. 121.

32. Cf. Mowinckel, in *Von Ugarit nach Qumran*, p. 140.

33. Cf. Noth, *System*, p. 8, n. 1; Zobel, *Stammesspruch und Geschichte*, pp. 4ff.; Schunck, *Benjamin*, pp. 13f., 71; Eissfeldt, *Introduction*, p. 228; Stoebe, in *RGG³* 3, cols. 524f.; Albright, *Yahweh and the Gods of Canaan*, pp. 17f., 230f.

34. Cf. Lindblom, in VTS 1, pp. 78ff. The latter translates 'until he come to Shiloh', i.e., the kingdom established will not be limited to Judah, but will extend also to the northern tribes, for which Shiloh, as a venerable site in Ephraim, is taken as the representative; cf. also von Rad, *Old Testament Theology* 2, pp. 12f.; Emerton, in *Words and Meanings*, pp. 86ff. However, cf. also Zobel, *Stammesspruch und Geschichte*, p. 55.

35. Cf. Noth, *System*, pp. 80f.; *idem, History of Israel*, pp. 58ff.

36. Cf. especially, Täubler, *Biblische Studien*, pp. 176ff.; Kaiser, *VT* 10, 1960, pp. 7ff., 10ff.; de Vaux, *Histoire*, pp. 589f. The expression 'house of Joseph' cannot, according to de Vaux, be traced back earlier than the monarchy. It should be understood as a parallel expression to 'house of Judah'.

37. Cf. Ottoson, *Gilead*, pp. 136ff.

38. Cf. Noth, *System*, p. 36; *idem, History of Israel*, pp. 61f.; Hoftijzer, *NedTTs* 14, 1959–60, p. 243.

39. Cf. below p. 96 and n. 33.

40. Cf. Noth, *Die israelitischen Personennamen*, p. 64.

41. It is often pointed out that Gen. 49.22 probably contains a play on the name Ephraim (on the verse cf. Emerton, in *Words and Meanings*, pp. 91ff.). However, it seems unlikely that it should be concluded from this that Joseph in Gen. 49 is synonymous with Ephraim and does not presuppose the rise of the tribe of Manasseh and the relations with Machir. If that were the case it would have to be explained why a group called Joseph adopted a new name, Ephraim, after settlement, or why a nameless group settled in the land should have adopted two names.

42. Täubler, *Biblische Studien*, pp. 190ff., argued that the meaning of the tribal name Machir shows that this was an independent tribe which probably

settled in the Amarna period. It should be seen as having formed part of the old *habiru* known to have been active at this time. Therefore, as distinct from the tribe of Issachar which bears an analogous name, Machir should be seen as having sold itself into military service. The Song of Deborah shows that Machir occupied the northern part of the mountains of Ephraim. This would have included the plain of Dothan. However, Gen. 37.17 connects Joseph with Dothan, and for this reason, and also because of the close association of Joseph with Shechem, the strong possibility exists that Joseph was originally a Machirite figure belonging to this area. This has been taken up and developed by Kaiser, *VT* 10, 1960, pp. 8ff., who thinks that in time Machir declined in strength and was eventually merged into those parts of Ephraim which, having been forced northwards by Philistine pressure, came to constitute the independent tribe of Manasseh. In this way the figure of Joseph passed from Machir to Manasseh and then to Ephraim. For a similar view, cf. now de Vaux, *Histoire,* pp. 540f., 589ff., 595ff.

43. Against Noth, *System*, p. 36, cf. Hoftijzer, *NedTTs* 14, 1959–60, p. 252.

44. Except for Meroz. This name is an enigma, cf. Alt, *Kleine Schriften* 1, pp. 274ff., who thinks that Meroz was a former Canaanite city which had been absorbed into Manasseh, though its exact location is not known. Against this, however, cf. Täubler, *Biblische Studien*, pp. 193ff. One can only say that it was probably a city connected with Israel, lying somewhere in the neighbourhood of the place where the battle was fought; cf. also below p. 134, n. 21.

45. That such an identification could be made was doubted by Noth, *System*, p. 36, n. 1, and has been shown to be most unlikely by Hoftijzer, *NedTTs* 14, 1959–60, 244ff.; see also Noth, *ZDPV* 75, 1959, pp. 14ff., where it is argued that the name Gilead belonged to an area just south of the Jabbok, while Gad, which settled north of the Arnon, was the most southern Israelite settlement east of Jordan. For a comprehensive treatment, cf. Ottoson, *Gilead*.

46. For the structure of the Song of Deborah, cf. below pp. 89f.

47. Cf. below pp. 98ff.

48. In this we differ from Noth, *System*, p. 36, who holds that the author of the Song of Deborah never intended to give a full list of the tribes of Israel, and so the Song is of no value as a list of tribes. However, the intention of the author should be distinguished from the effect of what he did, and it is the latter which is important here; cf. also Hoftijzer, *NedTTs* 14, 1959–60, pp. 252ff.

49. Deut. 33, which also clearly has the aim of preserving the number twelve of the tribes, is also probably a compilation of originally independent sayings about the tribes. The compiler of Deut. 33 has included Levi but omitted Simeon. The reason for this omission cannot be given. It cannot have been because of the virtual disappearance of Simeon as an independent tribe, for the same was probably true of Reuben at this time. To preserve the number twelve of the tribes, Joseph is divided into Ephraim and Manasseh. Indeed, v. 17b is probably an addition to the original saying about Joseph in vv. 13ff., but this addition is probably by the compiler of Deut. 33 himself. No certain date can be assigned to Deut. 33, nor can its relation to the other tribal lists be established.

50. Cf. Noth, *System*, pp. 40, 77ff., 89; *idem, History of Israel*, pp. 64, 69ff., 76.

51. Cf. Noth, *The Old Testament World*, pp. 68f.

52. Compare Num. 26.6 and Josh. 7.18, and cf. the work of Noth referred to in the preceding note, and *idem, History of Israel*, pp. 63ff. Noth has argued that Reuben and Simeon were important tribes in Palestine in the time before the settlement of the house of Joseph, and formed part of an amphictyony of six tribes composed of the Leah group of tribes. However, the existence of this fixed group of six tribes is made doubtful now since, in view of what has been said above, the position of Levi is so uncertain; cf. also Hoftijzer, *NedTTs* 14, 1959–60, p. 259; Mowinckel, in *Von Ugarit nach Qumran*, pp. 135f.

53. Cf. Judg. 13.2; 18.2, 11, where Dan is no longer a 'tribe' but a 'family'.

54. Cf. *System*, pp. 40f.

55. Cf. Rahtjen, *JNES* 24, 1965, pp. 100ff. Rahtjen's attempt to show that there is more justification for speaking of a Philistine rather than a Hebrew amphictyony runs aground because of our lack of information on the Philistines. Although the five city-states probably acted together in face of common peril (I Sam. 29.2), we have no evidence from them of a regular festival at a common central sanctuary. That Gath was a member of the Philistine league is doubted by Kassis, *JBL* 84, 1965, pp. 259ff.

56. Cf. Rahtjen, *JNES* 24, 1965, pp. 100ff.; Anderson, in *Translating and Understanding the Old Testament*, p. 143; de Vaux, *HTR* 64, 1971., p. 422.

57. The significance of the numbers six and twelve is in fact discounted altogether by some scholars, cf. Orlinsky, in *Studies and Essays in Honor of A. A. Neuman*, p. 376, n. 1. According to Eissfeldt, in *CAH* II, ch. xxxiv, p. 17, this was simply a conventional numbering of the Israelite tribes which in reality were sometimes less and sometimes more than twelve. This is perhaps supported by the fact that there are Assyrian records on Syria and Palestine which speak of twelve kings even if there were really only eleven, cf. Schmitt, *Der Landtag von Sichem*, p. 8, with references. See also de Vaux, *HTR* 64, 1971, pp. 422f., for a number of examples from both the Old Testament and outside Israel which indicate the widespread use of the number twelve in a symbolic way to express completeness.

58. Cf. Noth, *System*, pp. 97f., 151ff.; *idem, History of Israel*, p. 98.

59. Cf. *History of Israel*, pp. 94f. Albright, however, *Archaeology and the Religion of Israel*, p. 103; *idem, From the Stone Age to Christianity*, pp. 281f., argues, in view of such passages as Josh. 18.1, that Shiloh alone was the central sanctuary. This is followed by Wright, *Shechem*, pp. 140f.; Bright, *A History of Israel*, pp. 161f.; Nielsen, *Shechem*, p. 36, n. 1. However, cf. Mowinckel, *Tetrateuch-Pentateuch-Hexateuch*, p. 74, who holds that Shiloh was substituted for Shechem in the late (P) source to which Josh. 18.1 belongs, because at the time of composition of this source Shechem was the Samaritan centre and so could not be given the honour of having been the central sanctuary of the good old days; cf. also Smend, *Yahweh War and Tribal Confederation*, pp. 95f.

60. On this, cf. particularly Irwin, *RB* 72, 1965, pp. 161ff.; de Vaux, *HTR* 64, 1971, pp. 425ff. The most important of these criteria is, of course, that the sanctuary should be acknowledged by all the tribes as central sanctuary. The other two criteria are problematical; the significance of the ark is a matter of

dispute, and if Perlitt, *Bundestheologie im Alten Testament*, is to be followed, there was certainly no covenant worship in this period. However, ark and covenant are included here for the sake of completeness since they figured strongly in Noth's theory of the amphictyonic organization of Israel.

61. Cf. Noth, *Überlieferungsgeschichtliche Studien*, p. 9; L'Hour, *RB* 69, 1962, pp. 18f.; Nielsen, *Shechem*, pp. 134f.

62. Cf. Noth, *Josua*, pp. 135f.; Schmitt, *Landtag von Sichem*, p. 16; Perlitt, *Bundestheologie im Alten Testament*, pp. 239ff.

63. Cf. Noth, *Josua*, p. 137; Rudolph, *Der 'Elohist' von Exodus bis Josua*, pp. 244f.

64. Cf. L'Hour, *RB* 69, 1962, p. 26; de Vaux, *HTR* 64, 1971, pp. 423ff. Noth, *System*, pp. 65ff., also accepted this view at first, but later modified it since it seemed to be a too simple solution to the problems of the Israelite settlement to take it that it was the Rachel tribes which, under Joshua, introduced Yahwism to the Leah tribes already living in the land; cf. his *History of Pentateuchal Traditions*, pp. 50f., where it is argued that those who experienced Egypt and the Exodus were later incorporated into a number of tribes and tribal groups. Similarly, Noth would deny the possibility of determining precisely what group experienced the event at Sinai.

65. Cf. especially Schmitt, *Landtag von Sichem*, pp. 34ff., 40ff., 45, 48, 90f., 92ff.

66. Cf. e.g., Albright, *Yahweh and the Gods of Canaan*, p. 93.

67. The subject of the parallels between extra-biblical texts and Old Testament covenant passages has been thoroughly treated by McCarthy, *Treaty and Covenant*, and also in his book *Old Testament Covenant*, to which reference should be made for further details. See also Gray, *Joshua, Judges and Ruth*, pp. 32ff.

68. Cf. von Rad, *The Problem of the Hexateuch and Other Essays*, pp. 1ff.

69. But cf. below pp. 48f.

70. On this, cf. Noth, *History of Pentateuchal Traditions*, pp. 46, 54ff., 79f., 82, 110f., 198ff.; Alt, *Essays*, pp. 54f. It is most unlikely that literary criticism will succeed in producing an 'original' version of vv. 2–13 which would not presuppose the Pentateuchal presentation.

71. Cf. Mendenhall, *BA* 25, 1962, p. 84. There is no real parallel between this and the Elijah story in I Kings 18.21, for in the latter it is more a question of who is God rather than of which God should be served. Pedersen, *Israel* III–IV, p. 672, n. 5, has pointed to Judg. 5.8 ('new gods were chosen') which he calls a 'characteristic expression from the time of transition'. However, for a very different rendering of this phrase, cf. Margulis, *VT* 15, 1965, pp. 66ff.

72. Cf. McCarthy, *Treaty and Covenant*, pp. 146ff.

73. For examples of the use of the introductory 'and now' after such a historical recital, cf. Gen. 24.49; Ex. 19.5; Num. 22.6; Deut. 4.1; 10.12; 26.10; I Sam. 10.19; II Sam. 7.25.

74. Cf. also Judg. 10.10–16. The latter is probably a deuteronomistic passage, cf. Noth, *Überlieferungsgeschichtliche Studien*, p. 53. Beyerlin, however, in *Tradition und Situation*, p. 27, thinks that it originated in preaching in the context of the covenant-breaking Yahweh community. On Gen. 35.2ff., cf. especially Alt, *Kleine Schriften* 1, pp. 79ff.

75. For proposals, cf. Nielsen, *ST* 8, 1955, pp. 103ff.; Schmitt, *Landtag von Sichem*, pp. 49ff.

76. Cf. Weiser, *Psalms*, pp. 33, 61; Beyerlin, *Kulttraditionen Israels*, p. 40. Alt, *Kleine Schriften* 1, pp. 84f., calls it the negative first part of an action which then in the second part found its positive climax in the promise by the whole people to worship Yahweh alone.

77. McCarthy, *Treaty and Covenant*, pp. 149f., detects prophetic influence in these verses.

78. While Schmitt, *Landtag von Sichem*, pp. 21f., is right in warning against relying too much on what can be gained from concordance studies, this last point, taken together with the others, is enough to establish the late date of this section.

79. So, for example, the stone is witness in vv. 25–27, while it is the people who are witnesses against themselves in v. 22.

80. On this cf. Schmitt, *Landtag von Sichem*, pp. 13f., 24, 76, 83f., 101. It seems that Perlitt, *Bundestheologie im Alten Testament*, pp. 239ff., has glossed over rather too easily the signs of disunity in this chapter, which mark out vv. 25–27 as a distinct unit. See also Muilenburg, *VT* 9, 1959, pp. 357f.

81. Cf. Schmitt, *Landtag von Sichem*, p. 21; L'Hour, *RB* 69, 1962, p. 30.

82. That the stone was inscribed with the divine law, as proposed by L'Hour, *RB* 69, 1962, p. 32; Koch, *The Growth of the Biblical Tradition*, p. 29; Baltzer, *The Covenant Formulary*, p. 27, is possible but quite uncertain. According to the Targum, 'this stone is to us like the two stone tablets of the covenant . . . for the words which are inscribed on it are like all the words of Yahweh which he has spoken with us' (quoted in Schmitt, *Landtag von Sichem*, p. 9). That such a written record could also be a witness is shown by Deut. 31.26b; cf. Beyerlin, *Sinaitic Traditions*, pp. 44, 60. However, Beyerlin (*ibid.*, p. 61) thinks that the stone was thought of in popular piety as Yahweh's dwelling place, and (*ibid.*, p. 43) that v. 26a is 'the aetiological explanation of a corresponding document in Shechem'.

83. Rowley, *From Joseph to Joshua*, pp. 127f., points to the 'curious duplication' in events which are attributed to both Jacob and Joshua, and he suggests that Josh. 24 'represents the transfer to Joshua of an older tradition of a covenant between Israelites and Canaanites, but in an appropriately altered form'. However, the fundamental differences between Gen. 34 and Josh. 24 make it very improbable that the one is simply a changed form of the other; cf. also Seebass, *Erzvater Israel*, pp. 93f., n. 36.

84. Cf. Schmitt, *Landtag von Sichem*, p. 84; Alt, *Kleine Schriften* 1, p. 191. According to Kaufmann, *The Religion of Israel*, p. 250, n. 6, however, Shechem had also been taken over by Israel during the conquest. The contrast between the citizens of Shechem and the 'men of Israel' in Judg. 9 means no more than the contrast between the Benjaminites and the men of Israel in Judg. 20–21.

85. Möhlenbrink, *ZAW* 56, 1938, pp. 254ff., prefers the LXX reading in Josh. 24.1 (cf. also v. 25) which would locate this event at Shiloh; but the LXX is clearly a 'harmonistic alteration with reference to 18.1, 10; 19.51; 21.2; 22.9, 12', cf. Holmes, *Joshua*, pp. 8, 78.

86. Cf. Judg. 20.3, 12ff.

87. Cf. Josh. 17.2.

88. Cf. also Steuernagel in *Festschrift Georg Beer*, pp. 3ff.; Nielsen, *Shechem*, p. 139. Deut. 27 cannot be held to show a connection of the twelve tribes with Shechem in the period of the judges. There has been a secondary extension of a series of ten curses to the present series of twelve (cf. Nielsen, *The Ten Commandments in New Perspective*, p. 16), and the preceding verses are the result of the work of at least two different editors, which does not harmonize either with the curses of Deut. 27 or with the context of this chapter within Deuteronomy, cf. Nicholson, *Deuteronomy and Tradition*, pp. 21, 34; Schmitt, *Landtag von Sichem*, pp. 73f.

89. Cf. Davies, in *Promise and Fulfilment*, p. 61.

90. So Noth, *Josua*, pp. 51ff.; Soggin, *ZAW* 73, 1961, pp. 83f.; though cf. Noth, *Überlieferungsgeschichtliche Studien*, p. 43, where Josh. 8.30–35 is taken as wholly deuteronomistic with no older source.

91. L'Hour, *RB* 69, 1962, pp. 179ff., takes the passage as post-deuteronomistic. The important verse of this section, from our present point of view, is v. 33, since it is only here that the ark is mentioned; with its representation of the 'levitical priests' as the bearers of the ark, this verse, at least, would seem to be deuteronomistic, cf. Cody, *Old Testament Priesthood*, pp. 138ff.

92. Cf. Noth, *History of Israel*, p. 93, n. 1; Irwin, *RB* 72, 1965, p. 171.

93. Cf. Noth, *History of Israel*, pp. 94f.

94. Cf. Noth, *Überlieferungsgeschichtliche Studien*, p. 54, n. 2.

95. Cf Noth, *System*, pp. 162f.

96. Noth, *System*, p. 163, takes v. 5 to belong with these verses, but cf. Schunck, *Benjamin*, p. 59.

97. Cf. I Sam. 11.1ff., and Noth, *System*, pp. 163f.

98. Cf. Noth, *System*, p. 166; against Schunck, *Benjamin*, p. 65, n. 55. The clearest example of this borrowing is to be seen in a comparison of Judg. 20.36b–41 and Josh. 8. Schunck's denial of such borrowing is based on the expressions used for 'Israelites' which are different in Judg. 20.36b–41 and Josh. 8. However, on Schunck's use of this same argument in order to distinguish the basic text of Judg. 20 from additions to it, see the following note.

99. So also Schunck, *Benjamin*, p. 61. However, while the latter agrees that two independent sources do not exist here, he does argue for a much more extensive editing of the text than does Noth. Moreover, while Noth thinks of isolated and in most cases unconnected additions to the basic story, Schunck finds it possible to distinguish in Judg. 20 a series of additions which are consistent enough to be the work of one redactor. The criterion adopted by Schunck to separate this work of the redactor from the older basis is the use of *bᵉnê yiśrā'ēl* over against *'îš yiśrā'ēl*. The latter is the expression used in the older basis which is now supplemented. However, it seems very doubtful that this can work. The expression *bᵉnê yiśrā'ēl* (and *bᵉnê binyāmin*) does occur in what Schunck calls the older basic story, cf. Judg. 19.12, 30a; 20.3b, 24, 25a (also 20.24, 48). To explain these occurrences as due to the influence of the redactor simply illustrates the weakness of the criterion. But over and beyond this, Schunck's treatment involves the ascription to the redactor of long additions which cannot otherwise be justified, whereas there still remain suspect verses in what is taken as the basis edited by the redactor, cf. e.g., Judg. 20.42–46, and Noth, *System*, pp. 167f.

100. Danell, *Studies in the Name Israel*, p. 72, argues that since weeping is otherwise associated with Bethel, it is this place which should be understood in v. 23, and which then belongs to the basic story. However, the texts on which Danell relies are far from reliable. In Hos. 12.5 (EVV v. 4) it is not clear whether the weeping of Jacob belongs to Penuel or to Bethel, while the use of Judg. 2.4f. depends on an identification of Bochim with Bethel which is not beyond dispute (cf. the references in Danell, *ibid.*, p. 68, n. 60). Moreover, even if Danell is right in using these passages in this way, this does not mean that Bethel was exclusively the place for lamentation.

101. On the setting up of the royal sanctuaries, cf. I Kings 12.26ff.

102. Cf. Noth, *Überlieferungsgeschichtliche Studien*, p. 54, n. 2.

103. Cf. Judg. 17.7ff.; 19.1ff.

104. Cf. Judg. 17.6; 21.25; cf. also 18.1; 19.1.

105. On this, cf. particularly Noth, in *Israel's Prophetic Heritage*, pp. 68ff.

106. Cf. also Schunck, *Benjamin*, pp. 62f.

107. We are not concerned at this point with the question of the originality of Mizpah in this story, for which cf. Schunck, *Benjamin*, pp. 59ff. At any rate, Mizpah belongs to an earlier stage in the growth of the narrative than does Bethel.

108. Cf. Noth, *System*, pp. 166f.

109. So against Newman, *The People of the Covenant*, p. 60, n. 32; Clements, *Prophecy and Covenant*, p. 91, n. 2. Zobel, *Stammesspruch und Geschichte*, p. 118, n. 223, argues that Bethel is the original place of the assembly of the tribes in this story. Otherwise it is impossible to explain why it should have come in secondarily, since the only time it attained significance was in the time of Jeroboam I and then a reference to the ark would be an anachronism. However, it seems that one must distinguish between the information that Bethel was the gathering place of the tribes and the information that Bethel was where the ark was lodged. The former note is intended simply to show Bethel as an ancient sanctuary, which would suit well in the period of Jeroboam, while the latter is supporting information which probably rests on historical tradition. Smend, *Yahweh War and Tribal Confederation*, pp. 93f., also distinguishes between these two items of information about Bethel, but he does not attach any historical value to Judg. 20.27b, 28a. Soggin, *ZAW* 73, 1961, p. 80, argues that the terror of God, mentioned in Gen. 35.5, is found associated with the ark, and that therefore the ark was at both Shechem and Bethel and its transfer is reflected in this passage. However, the word *ḥittaṭ* in Gen. 35.5 only occurs in this passage, while cognate words occur in contexts which have nothing to do with the ark; cf. also Smend, *Yahweh War and Tribal Confederation*, p. 95.

110. Cf. Alt, *Kleine Schriften* 1, pp. 79ff.

111. Cf. Kraus, *VT* 1, 1951, p. 193; *idem, Worship in Israel*, pp. 164f. According to Kraus, Deut. 11.29f. may reflect the transfer of a Shechemite ceremony to Gilgal. However, this passage is extremely obscure, and even if the words 'opposite Gilgal' in v. 30 are to be claimed as original, and not rather as an addition (cf. Noth, *System*, p. 146; Nielsen, *Shechem*, pp. 42f.), the passage will hardly bear the interpretation given by Kraus.

112. Thus, Judg. 2.1a, 5b are said to reflect the transfer of the ark from

Gilgal to Bethel, cf. Zobel, *Stammesspruch und Geschichte*, p. 109, with references; and Danell, *Studies in the Name Israel*, p. 68 and n. 60 for the conjectural identification of Bochim with Bethel.

113. So Mowinckel, *Tetrateuch-Pentateuch-Hexateuch*, p. 36; but in this case the aetiological factor is probably secondary, cf. Bright, *Early Israel in Recent History Writing*, p. 97.

114. Cf. Mowinckel, *Tetrateuch-Pentateuch-Hexateuch*, pp. 36, 58.

115. Cf. Mowinckel, *ibid.*, p. 36. The parallel which Irwin, *RB* 72, 1965, pp. 172f., draws between this passage and Ex. 23.20ff. can certainly not be pressed as far as to take Josh. 5.13ff. as evidence of the covenant worship of Yahweh at Gilgal.

116. Cf. Irwin, *RB* 72, 1965, pp. 172f.; see also Lohfink, *Das Hauptgebot*, pp. 176ff.

117. Cf. Moore, *Judges*, p. 57.

118. Cf. Hvidberg, *Weeping and Laughter in the Old Testament*, pp. 105f.

119. Cf. Nicholson, *Deuteronomy and Tradition*, p. 62.

120. Cf. Noth, *Überlieferungsgeschichtliche Studien*, p. 5, n. 2. This same deuteronomistic device is also to be found, for example, in Josh. 23 where it is a speech by Joshua, and in I Kings 8 where it is a speech by Solomon. These speeches were composed to mark important transitional periods of Israel's history considered particularly significant by the deuteronomist.

121. So against Weiser, *Samuel*, pp. 82ff. For the covenant language of I Sam. 12, cf. Muilenburg, *VT* 9, 1959, pp. 360f.

122. Cf. Irwin, *RB* 72, 1965, pp. 172f.; for locating the cultic creed at Gilgal, Irwin relies on von Rad, *The Problem of the Hexateuch*, pp. 43ff.

123. Cf. von Rad, *The Problem of the Hexateuch*, p. 44.

124. For this, cf. Noth, *Josua*, pp. 11f.

125. On this, cf. Clements, *Abraham and David*, pp. 25ff.

126. The neutral designation 'historical summary' should probably be substituted for 'creed' in describing this form, cf. Hyatt, in *Translating and Understanding the Old Testament*, p. 164.

127. References at this point could be multiplied; but for a convenient summary of the position, with the necessary bibliography, cf. Hyatt, in *Translating and Understanding the Old Testament*, pp. 152ff.

128. Cf. Barr, *Old and New in Interpretation*, pp. 65ff., 74 and n. 1.

129. Cf. Hyatt, in *Translating and Understanding the Old Testament*, pp. 157f.; Childs, VTS 16, 1967, pp. 30ff.; Carmichael, *VT* 19, 1969, pp. 273ff.; see also the discussion of Josh. 24.2–13 above.

130. Cf. Möhlenbrink, *ZAW* 56, 1938, p. 248; Keller, *ZAW*, 68, 1956, p. 91; and, more recently, Maiser, *Das altisraelitische Ladeheiligtum*, pp. 21ff.

131. Cf. Noth, *Josua*, p. 33. As Noth points out, the story of the crossing of the Jordan could have been related without reference to the ark, just as the crossing of the Reed Sea is related in Josh. 4.23.

132. Cf. also Smend, *Yahweh War and Tribal Confederation*, p. 92. So against Maier, *Ladeheiligtum*, pp. 21ff. Maier manages to work out four successive recensions of two originally independent aetiological stories. The ark is taken as belonging to the third recension. Maier, *ibid.*, pp. 43ff., 57ff., thinks that the ark was manufactured at Shiloh as the symbol of an anti-Philistine tribal

alliance; but for a rather different account of its origin, cf. Beyerlin, *Sinaitic Traditions*, pp. 114ff.

133. It is, in fact, suggested by Cody, *Old Testament Priesthood*, p. 85, that at the end of the period of the judges the amphictyonic sanctuary was to be found at Nob. It is at Nob that the descendants of Eli appear in the time of Saul.

134. Cf. Wildberger, *Jahwes Eigentumsvolk*, pp. 65ff. However, because of the twelve stones element of the story of Josh. 3–4, Wildberger does think that Gilgal had significance for all Israel; on this, see further below.

135. For this, cf. especially Maier, *Ladeheiligtum*, pp. 21ff. With the latter's reconstruction I am in substantial agreement, except for his view of Josh. 4.9; see below n. 138.

136. This has been proposed by Kraus, *VT* 1, 1951, pp. 181ff.; *idem*, *Worship in Israel*, pp. 156ff. See also Soggin, *Joshua*, pp. 150ff.; Porter, *SEÅ* 36, 1971, pp. 5ff.

137. Cf. Noth, *Josua*, p. 33. This does not, of course, exclude the possibility that the tradition of the crossing of the Reed Sea has influenced the presentation of the story of the crossing of the Jordan. Such influence is to be seen especially in, for example, Josh. 4.10b, 23.

138. Maier, *Ladeheiligtum*, p. 23, is probably correct in seeing the original tradition of the crossing of the Jordan in Josh. 3.14a, 16, apart from two glosses: 'and rose up in a heap far off, at Adam, the city that is beside Zarethan', and 'the Salt Sea.' On the other hand, it does not seem to me to be correct to claim Josh. 4.9 as the original conclusion of this tradition. Josh. 4.9 is most likely a quite independent stone aetiology.

139. It is quite likely that the latter group of stones did not number twelve, but that this number was carried over from the aetiology of the Gilgal stones.

140. So Maier, *Ladeheiligtum*, p. 24, n. 159; see also Driver, in *Promise and Fulfilment*, p. 66.

141. Mizpah appears in Judg. 19–21 as an assembly place of the tribes. However, even if this is original, which is very doubtful, our treatment below (pp. 80f.) of these chapters shows that it is unlikely that all the tribes of Israel were involved in this event. Moreover, apart from this passage, Mizpah appears as a sanctuary only in the late anti-monarchic tradition in I Sam. 7.6; 10.17; cf. Noth, *Überlieferungsgeschichtliche Studien*, pp. 54f. Schunck, *Benjamin*, p. 60, conjectures that Mizpah was the home of the deuteronomist, who is responsible for its introduction into the Books of Judges and Samuel. On Mizpah, cf. also Muilenburg, *ST* 8, 1955, pp. 25ff.

142. Cf. above p. 117 n. 59.

143. The history of Shiloh itself from this time on has, until recently, evidently been the subject of some confusion. As a result of the Danish excavations there in 1926, it was thought that, having been destroyed by the Philistines on the occasion of the battle at Aphek, Shiloh remained unoccupied through the monarchy period, and that Jer. 7.12 alluded to this destruction, cf. Kjaer, *PEQ* 59, 1927, pp. 202ff.; Albright, *Archaeology and the Religion of Israel*, p. 104. However, as a result of the latest series of Danish excavations (cf. already Cody, *Old Testament Priesthood*, p. 110, n. 5), it is now clear that earlier conclusions were based on a false chronological reckoning, that there

is no archaeological (or, indeed, biblical) evidence for a destruction of Shiloh in this early time, and that Jer. 7.12 must refer to a more recent event, cf. Buhl and Holm-Nielsen, *Shiloh*, pp. 56ff., 6off.; Pearce, *VT* 23, 1973, pp. 105ff.

144. Cf. also Maier, *Ladeheiligtum*, p. 43.

145. Cf. above p. 117, n. 59.

146. Cf. above p. 44. The reference to Shiloh in Judg. 21.12 probably came into this context after the aetiological story in vv. 16ff. was connected with what precedes.

147. So against Nicholson, *Deuteronomy and Tradition*, p. 61; Bright, *History*, p. 164.

148. Cf. Haran, *VT* 19, 1969, pp. 11ff. On I Sam. 1–3 cf. Willis, *ST* 26, 1972, pp. 33ff.

149. Smend, *Yahweh War and Tribal Confederation*, pp. 76ff. (cf. also Herrmann, *TLZ* 89, 1964, cols. 813ff.), dissociates the ark from the central sanctuary, except perhaps for the case of Shiloh at the end of the judges period. This is in line with Smend's thesis that 'holy war' (associated with the ark) and 'amphictyony' represent two originally independent institutions which only came together gradually in the course of the period of the judges.

150. Since the ark in its travels did not go beyond the boundaries of Ephraim in the time before its capture by the Philistines, it is possible that in this time it was a particularly Ephraimite cult object visited by pilgrims from the tribe of Ephraim only.

151. Cf. above p. 34.

152. Cf. Noth, *System*, pp. 102f., n. 2. Noth includes also the words ʿēḏāh and qāhāl in this connection.

153. Mowinckel, *Le décalogue*, p. 31, argues that the title book of the covenant for this collection in Ex. 20.22–23.33 is misleading since no independent compilation, such as this title suggests, ever existed; cf. also *idem, ASTI* 2, 1963, p. 24, n. 14. However, while it is true that there are some later passages in this section, such as 23.20–33 which is probably deuteronomistic (cf. Noth, *Überlieferungsgeschichtliche Studien*, p. 13, n. 1; Beyerlin, *Sinaitic Traditions*, p. 5; though against this, cf. Brekelmans, VTS 15, 1966, p. 95), it seems more likely that a basic nucleus did once exist as an independent compilation to which these additions were made, than that the whole collection simply grew up gradually within its present context.

154. Proposals for a later date of compilation have been adequately dealt with by Weiser, *Introduction*, pp. 121ff.; cf. also Nielsen, *The Ten Commandments in New Perspective*, p. 78; Horst, in *RGG*[3] 1, col. 1525.

155. *System*, pp. 98f.

156. Cf. also Porter, *Moses and Monarchy*, p. 18, n. 57; Orlinsky, in *Studies and Essays in Honor of A. A. Neuman*, p. 379, n. 2. According to Speiser, *CBQ* 25, 1963, pp. 111ff., the *nāśī*' was the chosen leader of a tribal alliance, while Cazelles, *Études sur le code de l'alliance*, pp. 81f., 137f., thinks that the office of *nāśī*' was that of judge. It was something analogous to the position of the nomadic sheikh (so also de Vaux, *HTR* 64, 1971, p. 432) charged with deciding the affairs of the clan; but since the institution had no deep roots in Israel, it fell out of use during the period of the monarchy, to be revived again in the time of Ezekiel, a time of restoration and care for ancient ways. On Ex. 22.27

cf. also Phillips, *Ancient Israel's Criminal Law*, p.160; and on the *nāśī'*, cf. also van der Ploeg, *RB* 57, 1950, pp.40ff.

157. Cf. Mendenhall, *BA* 17, 1954, p.35, n.30, who remarks that hardly anything in the book of the covenant demands a legal unit larger than a village.

158. de Vaux, *HTR* 64, 1971, p.434, has rightly pointed out that the Greek amphictyony had no comparable office; the tribal representative exercised a certain judicial function. However, if an office of judge of Israel existed, it would presuppose an organization of the tribes which could be compared with the amphictyony.

159. Cf. McKenzie, *VT* 17, 1967, pp.119f.

160. On this cf. Noth, in *Bertholet Festschrift*, p.406; *idem, Überlieferungs-geschichtliche Studien*, pp.48f.

161. That Jephthah the judge and Jephthah the deliverer were really two different men is unlikely; they are both called Gileadite; cf. Noth, *Über-lieferungsgeschichtliche Studien*, pp.48f., n.5.

162. Cf. Noth, *History of Israel*, p.101; *idem, Überlieferungsgeschichtliche Studien*, p.49; Beyerlin, in *Tradition und Situation*, p.7.

163. Cf. Schmidt, *Königtum Gottes in Ugarit und Israel*, pp.28ff.; Fensham, *OTWerkSuidA* 1959, pp.15ff.; van Selms, *OTWerkSuidA* 1959, pp.41ff. Schmidt finds the meaning 'rule' for *špṭ* by referring to the cognate Ugaritic word *ṭpṭ*, which is found in parallelism with *zbl* 'prince' and *mlk* 'king'. Furthermore, he argues that the meaning 'rule' suits best with the context of the enthronement psalms, in Pss.96.13; 98.9. See also Richter, *ZAW* 77, 1965, pp.57ff., who follows Schmidt, and (*ibid.*, pp.61ff.) discovers further support in the Mari tablets and in Phoenician-Punic material. For I Sam. 8.5,6,20, cf. Hertzberg, *ZAW* 40, 1922, p.257. However, it does not seem possible to prove either from these passages or from the others noted by Hertzberg, which use the verb *špṭ* in connection with the activites of leaders in Israel, that the original meaning of the root is 'rule' from which the meaning 'judge' is derived. The fact that a ruler was also responsible for the mainten-ance of justice in itself says little about the original meaning of the root.

164. Cf. Grether, *ZAW* 57, 1939, p.114 (with reference to Dan.9.12 (*bis*); Amos 2.3); see also Smend, *Yahweh War and Tribal Confederation*, pp.47f.

165. Cf. also Pss.72.4; 82.3; and Köhler-Baumgartner, *Lexicon in Veteris Testamenti Libros*, s.v. *špṭ* 3, p.1003; cf. also Köhler, *Hebrew Man*, pp.156f.

166. The section on Othniel in Judg.3.7ff. is obscure and may be wholly deuteronomistic, cf. Noth, *Überlieferungsgeschichtliche Studien*, p.51, n.1; Smend, *Yahweh War and Tribal Confederation*, p.75, n.129. It does not conform with the information given on Othniel in Josh.15.15ff. Depending on the traditions in which Joshua and Samuel are taken to be original, it is possible that they are exceptions to the statement that the names of the charismatic deliverers have been preserved because of their exploits related in the traditions about them; Joshua acts as a judge in Josh.7, while there are also other occasional indications of a connection of charisma and judicial functions, cf. Rendtorff, in *History and Hermeneutic*, p.30; Noth, *The Laws in the Pentateuch*, pp.242f. However, because a leader exercised judicial functions on occasions, it cannot be concluded that he was a judge like those of the list. On Samuel, see further below.

167. In the context of the charismatic deliverers, the root *špṭ* appears only in the framework passages in Judg. 2.16ff.; 3.10 (cf. also previous note); and 15.20.

168. This is true even of Tola, of whom it is recorded in Judg. 10.1 that he arose 'to deliver Israel'. This expression is here most likely to be taken as deuteronomistic, cf. Smend, *Yahweh War and Tribal Confederation*, pp. 53, 75, n. 129.

169. For what follows see especially Schunck, VTS 15, 1966, pp. 252ff.

170. Schunck, VTS 15, 1966, p. 253 and n. 3, argues that in Judg. 10.1 the word 'after' originally read 'after him' (the change, together with the addition of 'Abimelech' being the work of the deuteronomistic redactor), so that there must have been at least one judge before Tola. However, it is just as likely that 'after' is to be taken along with 'Abimelech' as an addition, and that 'and there arose' constituted the beginning of the list (on the expression 'to deliver Israel' as deuteronomistic here, cf. previous note but one).

171. Noth, *Überlieferungsgeschichtliche Studien*, p. 52, n. 1, however, thinks that 'and there arose' in Judg. 10.1, 3 was brought in by the deuteronomist following on the use of this verb to describe the rise of the charismatic deliverers.

172. Cf. Schunck, VTS 15, 1966, pp. 254ff.

173. For Joshua as judge, cf. also Smend, *Yahweh War and Tribal Confederation*, pp. 53f.

174. As has happened with Jephthah, so also with Samuel, the first element of the literary form may have been suppressed as a result of the incorporation of other material and the consequent separation of Samuel from his place in the list.

175. Cf. Hertzberg TLZ 79, 1954, cols. 285ff.; *idem*, *Die Bücher Josua, Richter, Ruth*, pp. 209f. Hertzberg would also include Abimelech. Against the view that Deborah should be reckoned as a judge, cf. Richter, *Traditionsgeschichtliche Untersuchungen zum Richterbuch*, pp. 41f. Quite apart from Deborah, the place of Joshua is also a problem. For different views on the tradition to which he originally belongs, cf. Alt, *Kleine Schriften* 1, pp. 187ff.; Noth, *Josua*, p. 61.

176. Cf. Noth, *Überlieferungsgeschichtliche Studien*, pp. 47ff.

177. On Samuel, see further below.

178. Cf. Richter, *Richterbuch*, p. 237, who suggests this as a possibility for Gideon.

179. Cf. above, and von Rad, *Old Testament Theology* 1, p. 331, n. 7. It seems to me unlikely that the deuteronomist understood the deliverers as 'real' judges. He simply applied to them the word *špṭ* in a different, but still frequent, sense, in order to present a uniform picture of the period with which he was dealing. According to Thomson, *TGUOS* 19, 1961–62, pp. 74ff., the root *špṭ* refers to the ascertaining of the divine will with regard to the matter at hand, and *mišpāṭ* is the divine decision. This would perhaps suit the case of Deborah in Judg. 4.4f. and a few other instances outside the Book of Judges (for which cf. Noth, *The Laws in the Pentateuch*, pp. 242f.); but it is unlikely that this is true of other uses of the root in the Book of Judges, especially since (*a*) it can hardly be claimed as a usual sense of the root; and (*b*) it is not particularly suggested by the traditions available. See also McKenzie, *The World of the Judges*, pp. 16, 117f.

180. Noth, in *Bertholet Festschrift*, pp. 404ff.

181. Cf. Noth, in *Bertholet Festschrift*, p. 415. On the continued existence of the amphictyony throughout the period of the monarchy, with Jerusalem as the central sanctuary, cf. Noth, *The Laws in the Pentateuch*, pp. 28ff. This is followed up and developed by Beyerlin, *Kulttraditionen Israels*, pp. 25ff. However, cf. von Rad, *Studies in Deuteronomy*, p. 64, n. 2.

182. Cf. Noth, in *Bertholet Festschrift*, p. 414, n. 1; *idem, Überlieferungsgeschichtliche Studien*, p. 48.

183. For others, cf. Beyerlin, *Kulttraditionen Israels*, pp. 17ff.; Willis, *VT* 18, 1968, pp. 529ff.

184. Cf. Beyerlin, *Kulttraditionen Israels*, pp. 18f.

185. The translation of Micah 4.14a is, however, disputed; cf. Willis, *VT* 18, 1968, pp. 533f.

186. Beyerlin, *Kulttraditionen Israels*, p. 14, translates Micah 1.15b 'he (i.e. the enemy) is coming to Adullam, O glory of Israel', and takes 'O glory of Israel' as a reference to Jerusalem.

187. Willis, *VT* 18, 1968, pp. 532f.

188. See also Beyerlin, *Kulttraditionen Israels*, pp. 19f.; Willis, *VT* 18, 1968, p. 533; cf. also Porteous, in *Tradition und Situation*, p. 96; McKenzie, *VT* 17, 1967, p. 121; Kraus, *Worship in Israel*, pp. 188f.; Bächli, *Israel und die Völker*, pp. 187, 189f.; Phillips, *Ancient Israel's Criminal Law*, pp. 20f.

189. Cf. e.g., II Sam. 12.1ff.; 14.2ff. Also in Isa. 16.5 and II Kings 15.5, the Davidic king is one who 'judges' the people.

190. On this passage, cf. above p. 125, n. 163.

191. However, for a different interpretation of these verses, cf. Alt, *Essays*, p. 228, n. 149. On the general subject of the king's responsibility for justice, cf. also Ps. 122.3–5 and Horst, *Gottes Recht*, pp. 264f.; and Ps. 101 with the remarks of Johnson, *Sacral Kingship*, p. 116, n. 1. See also Johnson, in *Myth, Ritual and Kingship*, pp. 206f.; Clements, *Prophecy and Covenant*, p. 73. I Sam. 8.5, 20 (cf. also I Sam. 10.25) may indicate the transfer to the king of the judicial functions formerly exercised by Samuel, cf. McKenzie, *VT* 17, 1967, p. 121.

192. On this, cf. Köhler, *Hebrew Man*, pp. 149ff.

193. Noth, *Überlieferungsgeschichtliche Studien*, pp. 49f.

194. Cf. Schunck, *VTS* 15, 1966, p. 258, n. 1.

195. On the other hand, the representation of Samuel as a deliverer, in I Sam. 7; 12.11, is clearly a deuteronomistic construction, cf. Noth, *Überlieferungsgeschichtliche Studien*, pp. 55, 59; Smend, *Yahweh War and Tribal Confederation*, p. 71. Weiser, *Samuel*, pp. 17ff., 79ff., finds covenant language in these chapters, but takes no account of their deuteronomistic character.

196. This old Samuel tradition now stands in a deuteronomistic context, cf. Noth, *Überlieferungsgeschichtliche Studien*, pp. 55, 60.

197. There were several places in Palestine bearing the name Mizpah, or Mizpeh, which is hardly surprising in view of the meaning of the name – 'outlook point'. The one mentioned here is probably to be identified with Tell en-Nasbeh, about seven miles north of Jerusalem, or with Nebi Samwil, about five miles north of Jerusalem, cf. Noth, *The Old Testament World*, p. 137. All the places mentioned in I Sam. 7.16, with the possible exception of Mizpah (for which, see above p. 123 n. 141), were sanctuaries.

198. Irwin, *RB* 72, 1965, p.182, has suggested that Samuel's circuit should be seen in the light of Ex.23.14–17, that is, Samuel visited each sanctuary in turn at the time of one of the three festivals when a large number of Israelites would be present. But such a connection is nowhere suggested by the tradition, and is further weakened by the uncertainty on the place of Mizpah as a sanctuary.

199. Cf. Smend, *Yahweh War and Tribal Confederation*, p.70.

200. The information in I Sam.8.1 that Samuel appointed his sons 'judges for Israel' when he himself was old, which implies that they followed their father in a position of significance for all Israel, would then be the work of the editor who understood these judges to have something more than local importance.

201. An exception to this is Tola who, though belonging to the tribe of Issachar, lived, and probably also judged, in Ephraim. Whatever the reason for this may have been, it does not in any way support the view that these judges had significance and influence for all Israel.

202. It is this which must have given rise to the present formulation of Deut.17.9. Even if Noth, *Bertholet Festschrift*, p.416, n.4, is right in saying that Deut.19.17, where the plural 'judges' is used, is secondary in relation to Deut.17.9 (though in view of II Chron.19.8–11 this cannot be certain), the time gap would prohibit the use of Deut.17.9 to elucidate the nature and function of the 'judge of Israel', cf. also Smend, *Yahweh War and Tribal Confederation*, pp.45f.; Phillips, *Ancient Israel's Criminal Law*, p.22, n.41.

203. So Richter, *ZAW* 77, 1965, p.57.

204. Cf. Mendenhall, in *Biblical Studies in Memory of H. C. Alleman*, p.90, n.4; Eissfeldt, in *CAH* II ch.xxxiv, p.20. The latter's view that Jair is the personification of a group is hardly tenable. The number of years of office assigned to each judge encourages confidence in their having been individuals, and if the other judges are individuals then probably Jair is also; cf. Noth, in *Bertholet Festschrift*, pp.412f.

205. So against Schunck, VTS 15, 1966, pp.259f.

206. On the basis of an Icelandic parallel, Alt, *Essays*, pp.102f., thinks that the judge proclaimed the casuistic law adopted from the Canaanites. On the other hand, however, it has also been argued that the judge proclaimed the divine law to the people and that his office, or at least this aspect of it, was taken over by the prophets who acted as 'covenant mediators', cf. Noth, *History of Israel*, pp.102f.; Beyerlin, *Kulttraditionen Israels*, pp.20f.; Kraus, *Die prophetische Verkündigung des Rechts in Israel*, pp.18f.; Muilenburg, in *The Bible in Modern Scholarship*, pp.74ff.

207. Cf. Richter, *ZAW* 77, 1965, p.71.

208. Cf. Noth, in *Alttestamentliche Studien Friedrich Nötscher zum 60. Geburtstag gewidmet*, p.163; Smend, *Yahweh War and Tribal Confederation*, p.46.

209. Even if Joshua is here represented as one who decided and fixed the borders of the tribes, it is most unlikely that he is to be claimed as a judge, cf. above p.60.

210. Cf. Alt, *Kleine Schriften* 1, pp.193ff.; Noth, in *Alttestamentliche Studien*, pp.152ff.; *idem, Josua*, pp.13ff.; von Rad, *Old Testament Theology* 1, p.299. See also Soggin, *Joshua*, pp.11ff.

211. Cf. Mowinckel, *Zur Frage nach dokumentarischen Quellen in Josua 13–19*, p. 16, who argues for the existence of an amphictyony of ten tribes which could not be the source of such a border system as we have in Josh. 13–19.

212. Cf. above p. 15.

213. Cf.Mowinckel, *Quellen in Josua 13–19*, p. 8. However, Mowinckel does not seem to be quite consistent in his argument, since later (*ibid.*, p. 11) he argues that we must reckon with a living tradition in Josh. 13–19.

214. Cf. Noth, in *Alttestamentliche Studien*, p. 158.

215. It is not necessary to go into much detail here on the vexed question of the presence of P in the Book of Joshua. Noth, *Überlieferungsgeschichtliche Studien*, pp. 180ff.; *idem*, *History of Pentateuchal Traditions*, pp. 8ff., argues that the priestly writing ended with the death of Moses and that the other Pentateuchal sources, which had originally told of the settlement in the land, were later curtailed in order to fit into the framework provided by P. Thus, Josh. 1–12 is to be treated as part of the deuteronomistic history, and Josh. 13–19 as an addition to this deuteronomistic work. None of the Pentateuchal sources is to be found in Joshua. In the light of Noth's position, Bright, *IB* 2, pp. 543f., seems rather inconsistent in his argument. He agrees with Noth: (*a*) that P is not to be found in Joshua; (*b*) that P formed the framework of the Pentateuchal sources. Yet, Bright also argues for the presence of JE in Josh. 1–12. However, it seems that Noth's view raises as many difficulties as it solves at this point. For if, on the question of the presence of P in Joshua, style and speech can no longer be taken as reliable criteria for distinguishing the presence of P (cf. Noth, *Überlieferungsgeschichtliche Studien*, p. 184), it is difficult to see on what basis P may be discerned at all. See further, Mowinckel, *Tetrateuch-Pentateuch-Hexateuch*, pp. 52ff., 55ff., 58ff.; Weiser, *Introduction*. pp. 146f.

216. So Kiriath-jearim and Beth-arabah are assigned in Josh. 15.60f. to Judah, and in Josh. 18.22, 28 to Benjamin; Eshtaol and Zorah are assigned in Josh. 15.33 to Judah, and to Dan in Josh. 19.41.

217. On this, cf. especially Alt, *Kleine Schriften* 2, pp. 276ff., who finds in this list twelve provinces into which the kingdom of Judah was divided in the time of Josiah; cf. also Noth, *Josua*, p. 14. According to Cross and Wright, *JBL* 75, 1956, pp. 222ff. (cf. also Bright, *IB* 2, p. 545; Gray, *Joshua, Judges and Ruth*, pp.24f.), the province list of Judah included only Josh. 15.21–62; 18.21–28, which goes back to the time of David, but was brought up to date under Jehoshaphat. It is argued by Aharoni, *VT* 9, 1959, pp. 225ff., that the Judean province list included Josh. 15.21–44, 48–62; 18.25–28, while 18.21–24 represents a fragment of a place list of the kingdom of Israel giving the Benjamin district of Israel; cf. also Grønbaek, *VT* 15, 1965, pp. 432f. At any rate, this city-list stands quite apart from the boundary lists and may be left out of consideration here.

218. Compare the actual figures given in vv. 15, 22, 30, 38, with the numbers of cities mentioned. The additions seem to have been taken from Josh. 21 and Judg. 1, cf. Noth, *Josua*, p. 114.

219. Cf. Alt, *ZAW* 45, 1927, pp. 59ff. The only one of the Galilean tribes about which it seems to me there could be any doubt on this is Zebulun, whose territory is described in Josh. 19.10–14. While Issachar is dealt with

simply by a list of cities, and Asher and Naphtali are determined both
with lists of cities and with reference to the other tribes which bordered them,
with a minimum of connecting text giving the impression of a border
description, Zebulun seems to have a genuine border description. But even
here the conclusion of the description of Zebulun's territory in v.16 is that
which is found with city-lists rather than with boundary descriptions.

220. Cf. Noth, *ZDPV* 58, 1935, pp.185ff.

221. So Noth, *Josua*, p.14; and, for further objections to Noth's fixed
border points as the basis of the border descriptions, cf. Mowinckel, *Quellen
in Josua13–19*.

222. Noth, *ZDPV* 58, 1935, pp.232ff., has attempted to make such a
distinction, and to derive the information of Josh.13 from two sources: one,
the city-lists, and, two, the boundary descriptions. But as with Josh.19, this
attempt is hardly justified since no such distinction is made in the text of
Josh.13 in the way that boundary descriptions and city-lists are distinguished
for Judah in Josh.15. Against Noth here, cf. also Glueck, *AASOR* 18–19,
1939, pp.249ff.

223. Cf. Hoftijzer, *NedTTs* 14, 1959–60, pp.245ff.; Noth, *ZDPV* 75, 1959,
pp.61f. and n.117. See also Soggin, *Joshua*, pp.154ff.

224. Cf. Schunck, *Benjamin*, pp.146ff., who argues that Josh.16.1–3
represents the northern border of the kingdom of Judah in the time of
Rehoboam. This not only accounts for the substantial repetition of this
border line in vv.5b–6a, but also explains why only the southern border of
the house of Joseph is given.

225. On these points, cf. Alt, *Kleine Schriften* 1, pp.194ff.

226. Cf. Alt, *Kleine Shriften* 1, pp.198ff.

227. On the historical course of events at this time, cf. above p.29. Alt,
Kleine Schriften 1, p.200, explains Josh.17.8 as showing the result of an
invasion by Manassite groups from the north into the area of Tappuah, which
did not involve taking the city itself. The city was later taken by Ephraimites
coming from the south. However, in the light of what we have already said
above p.29, it seems better to follow Täubler, *Biblische Studien*, p.190, in
understanding that after families of Ephraimites expanded to the north, they
did not all become part of the later tribe of Manasseh, but some retained their
identity as Ephraimites. This would most naturally have happened in the
Manassite area immediately adjoining Ephraim, and so Josh.17.9 can speak
of cities of Manasseh which belong to Ephraim.

228. Cf. Alt, *Essays*, pp.133ff., 171ff.

229. Cf. Noth, *Josua*, pp.109f.

230. Cf. Noth, in *Alttestamentliche Studien*, p.162.

231. Cf. Alt, *Kleine Schriften* 1, pp.196ff., followed by Noth, in *Alttestamentliche Studien*, p.162; *idem*, *Josua*, p.13.

232. Cf. von Rad, *The Problem of the Hexateuch*, pp.79ff.

233. Cf. Buccellati, *Cities and Nations of Ancient Syria*, pp.148ff.

234. Cf. also McKenzie, *The World of the Judges*, p.6.

235. von Rad, *Studies in Deuteronomy*, p.45.

236. Cf. above p.113, n.17.

237. For the most recent critical survey of theories on the course of the

settlement of the tribes, cf. Weippert, *The Settlement of the Israelite Tribes in Palestine*.

238. So Kraus, *Worship in Israel*, p. 137.

239. Cf. especially von Rad, *Der heilige Krieg im alten Israel*; also de Vaux, *Ancient Israel*, pp. 258ff.; Weippert, *ZAW* 84, 1972, pp. 46off.; Stolz, *Jahwes und Israels Kriege*.

240. It is unsuitable for two reasons; first, it obscures the essentially Yahwistic-Israelite nature of the wars and opens the way to treating them in the light of the holy wars practised elsewhere, cf. Richter, *Richterbuch*, p. 186; secondly, Smend (see below) has drawn a sharp distinction between the holy war and the 'amphictyonic war'. If it is right to treat the holy war as something quite apart from the question of the Israelite amphictyony, then the holy war should be given some other designation in the Israelite context; this is because the Greeks gave the designation 'holy wars' to their 'amphictyonic wars'. It would, therefore, perhaps be better to speak of the 'wars of Yahweh' rather than 'holy wars' in the Israelite context.

241. Against von Rad, *Der heilige Krieg*, p. 7, and de Vaux, *Ancient Israel*, p. 258, cf. Weiss, *HUCA* 37, 1966, p. 33, who remarks that the fact that David asked Uriah why he did not go down to his house (II Sam. 11.10) shows that sexual abstinence was not a requirement of the holy war.

242. On these, cf. particularly Richter, *Richterbuch*, pp. 177ff., who finds two main literary schemes used to describe the holy wars.

243. In a discussion of the pericope dealing with Gideon and the Midianite war, Beyerlin, *VT* 13, 1963, pp. 1ff., has argued that the present form of the Gideon tradition is due, not to holy war ideas, but to the influence of the covenant tradition in the framework of the amphictyony. The war with the Midianites has now been included in the *Heilsgeschichte*, so that it has now become an event concerning all Israel in which Yahweh effected deliverance without any help from Israel.

244. So, for example, it is not clear if a holy war could be a war of aggression (so Bright, *History*, p. 138, n. 73; Newman, *The People of the Covenant*, p. 102, n. 3), or was always a defensive war (so von Rad, *Der heilige Krieg*, p. 26; Graf Reventlow, *ZTK* 60, 1963, p. 293; Vriezen, *The Religion of Ancient Israel*, pp. 163ff.).

245. Cf. Smend. *Yahweh War and Tribal Confederation*, pp. 33ff., and *passim*.

246. Smend, *ibid.*, pp. 16ff., 29, 50f.

247. Smend, *ibid.*, pp. 43ff.

248. Smend, *ibid.*, pp. 76ff. Smend admits the integral connection between the ark and the holy war, but denies that the ark formed the amphictyonic central sanctuary.

249. Smend, *ibid.*, pp. 98ff.

250. Smend, *ibid.*, pp. 39, 117f.

251. While saying (*ibid.*, p. 27) that the amphictyony is no more than a theory, even if a probable one, Smend (*ibid.*, pp. 20f., 32) also argues that the cry for help in the holy war from one tribe to another is the clearest indication of an Israelite unity at this time which should be seen within the context of an amphictyony.

252. That one can think generally of a deuteronomistic framework to

these narratives in the Book of Judges, as proposed by Noth, *Überlieferungs-geschichtliche Studien*, pp. 47ff., is denied by Beyerlin, in *Tradition und Situation*, pp. 1ff. However, while Beyerlin may be correct in his argument that Judg. 2.11–19 is later than and presupposes the existence of other framework passages, it is still true that in the passages with which we are concerned here the framework is uniform and is the work of an editor (whoever such an editor may have been) who has gathered formerly independent traditions and set them in the sequence in which they are now to be found.

253. Cf. McKenzie, *The World of the Judges*, pp. 8f., 121f.

254. Against the argument of Noth, *Die israelitischen Personennamen*, p. 123, n. 1; and Albright, *From the Stone Age to Christianity*, p. 283, that 'son of Anath' means that Shamgar came from Beth-anath, cf. van Selms, *VT* 14, 1964, pp. 301ff. See also Aharoni, in *Near Eastern Archaeology in the Twentieth Century*, pp. 255f.; Eissfeldt, in *CAH* II ch. xxxiv, p. 22.

255. Judg. 4 and 5 are considered below pp. 84ff.

256. For an exhaustive treatment of the Gideon tradition from the literary, form-critical and traditio-historical points of view, cf. Richter, *Richterbuch*, pp. 112ff. On the relationship of Gideon and Jerubbaal, cf. also Täubler, *Biblische Studien*, pp. 265ff.; Haag, *ZAW* 79, 1967, pp. 305ff.

257. Judg. 6.35 is rejected by von Rad, *Der heilige Krieg*, pp. 22f., as an addition, but he accepts Judg. 7.23f. as showing the subsequent collective action of the tribes, and therewith 'amphictyonic interest' in the event. But if 6.35 is rejected there is no reason for accepting 7.23 as original, particularly in the light of 8.2; cf. also Beyerlin *VT* 13, 1963, p. 15.

258. Cf. Judg. 4.6. Tabor is claimed to have been an amphictyonic sanctuary by Alt, *Kleine Schriften* 2, p. 404, n. 4; Kraus, *Worship in Israel*, pp. 166ff.; von Rad, *Old Testament Theology* 1, p. 21.

259. Cf. Soggin, *Das Königtum in Israel*, pp. 23ff.; Linders, *JTS* 16, 1965, pp. 315ff.; but against this, cf. Kaufmann, *The Religion of Israel*, p. 253.

260. On the geographical details of this story, and especially on the double use of the name Gilead in Judg. 10.17; 11.29, cf. Noth, *ZDPV* 75, 1959, pp. 34ff.

261. On this as a deuteronomistic verse, cf. Noth, *Überlieferungsgeschichtliche Studien*, p. 53; Smend, *Yahweh War and Tribal Confederation*, p. 20.

262. It is true that in Judg. 11.29, just before the battle with the Ammonites, it is said that 'the spirit of the Lord came upon Jephthah'; but this, in view of the rest of the narrative, should be taken as an expression of the wish to make the case of Jephthah conform with that of the other deliverers; cf. von Rad, *Der heilige Krieg*, p. 24.

263. Cf. Noth, *Überlieferungsgeschichtliche Studien*, p. 61.

264. In Judg. 13.5 Manoah's wife receives the promise that the son who will be born to her will be a Nazirite who will 'begin to deliver Israel from the hand of the Philistines'.

265. Cf. e.g., Judg. 3.27; 7.24; 12.2, and Smend, *Yahweh War and Tribal Confederation*, pp. 20f.; von Rad, *Der heilige Kreig*, pp. 23, 25f.

266. The battle with the Philistines at Aphek, recorded in I Sam. 4, will be considered below pp. 94ff.

267. Cf. above pp. 42ff.

268. Cf. Noth, *System*, pp. 102f., n. 2.

269. Cf. also Smend, *Yahweh War and Tribal Confederation*, pp. 33f.

270. Cf. Schunck, *Benjamin*, p. 64.

271. So Schunck, *Benjamin*, p. 64. Such a use of this figure is also to be found in Ex. 18.21–25, according to which Moses divided the people on the basis of the number ten, and set judges over them in order to ease the burden on himself and facilitate the administration of justice; on this section, cf. Knierim, *ZAW* 73, 1961, pp. 146ff., who argues that vv. 21b, 25b, which refer to this division of the people, are based on military practice and are additions deriving from the time of Josiah.

272. Cf. above, pp. 43f.

273. Cf. Judg. 17.7ff. and Schunck, *Benjamin*, p. 66.

274. Cf. above p. 44.

275. Thus, Gen. 9.20–27 explains the subjection of the Canaanites to the Israelites and the Philistines, while Gen. 35.22 (cf. Gen. 49.3f.) explains the decline of the tribe of Reuben to insignificance, cf. Eissfeldt, in *Festschrift Georg Beer*, pp. 22f.; Gunkel, *What Remains of the Old Testament*, p. 159f. On what follows, cf. particularly Eissfeldt, in *Festschrift Georg Beer*, pp. 19ff.

276. Cf. Noth, *Josua*, pp. 11f. Noth takes the presence of Joshua in these traditions as secondary. It was as a result (*a*) of the Benjaminite conquest tradition being accepted as the conquest tradition of all Israel, and (*b*) of the place which Joshua occupied in the important covenant tradition (Josh. 24), that he was introduced into the originally Benjaminite conquest tradition.

277. Cf. above p. 114, n. 23.

278. A group called the 'Banu-jamina' corresponding to another group called the 'Banu-simal' is referred to in the Mari letters, cf. Schunck, *Benjamin*, pp. 6ff.; Noth, *Die Ursprünge des alten Israel im Lichte neuer Quellen*, p. 14; Gelb, *JCS* 15, 1961. pp. 37f. But a connection of the biblical Benjamin with the Banu-jamina of the Mari letters is extremely unlikely, cf. also Zobel, *Stammesspruch und Geschichte*, p. 112, n. 198a.

279. So against Noth, *History of Israel*, p. 74, n. 4; cf. Eissfeldt, in *CAH* II ch. xxxiv, pp. 11, 14; de Vaux, *Histoire*, pp. 587ff.

280. Eissfeldt. in *Festschrift Georg Beer*, pp. 19ff., sees a reference to Benjamin in the 'archers' of Gen. 49.22–26, but yet he concludes that Benjamin did succeed in setting itself up as an independent tribe on this occasion. However, it is clear from Judg. 20 that Ephraim was the victor in the battle, and also in Gen. 49 Joseph is successful against the 'archers', cf. Zobel, *Stammesspruch und Geschichte*, p. 117.

Chapter III

1. For an elaborate treatment of the Song of Deborah, cf. Richter, *Richterbuch*, pp. 65ff.

2. For this, cf. Weiser, *ZAW* 71, 1959, pp. 67ff., who follows Bentzen, *Introduction* 1, pp. 138ff. Weiser is followed by Schunck, *Benjamin*, p. 52; Beyerlin, *Sinaitic Traditions*, p. 79; Gray, *Joshua, Judges and Ruth*, pp. 219ff.

3. Cf. Weiser, *ZAW* 71, 1959, p. 73.

4. Cf. Judg. 4.6, 12.

5. Cf. Weiser, *ZAW* 71, 1959, p. 92.

6. This presupposes reading Naphtali for the second Issachar in v. 15, cf. Mowinckel, in *Von Ugarit nach Qumran*, p. 137, n. 15.

7. Compare, for example, the description of the theophany of Yahweh in Judg. 5.4f. with similar descriptions in Pss. 18.8ff. (EVV vv. 7ff.); 50.2ff.; 77.17ff. (EVV vv. 16ff.).

8. Cf. also Craigie, *JBL* 88, 1969, p. 254, n. 11.

9. Cf. Richter, *Richterbuch*. p. 29.

10. For what follows see especially Richter, *Richterbuch*, pp. 32ff., 61.

11. Cf. Richter, *Richterbuch*, pp. 55f., 62.

12. Judg. 4.17b, 23f., would also clearly belong to the same edition of this chapter which makes Jabin king of Canaan.

13. On this, cf. Noth, *Josua*, pp. 67ff.; and, for the significance of this event, cf. Alt, *Essays*, p. 168.

14. According to Ackroyd, *VT* 2, 1952, pp. 160ff., a period of about a century separates the event from the fully formed poetic record of it.

15. Cf. above, n. 7.

16. This excludes Ps. 68 of course, with which verbal parallels are to be seen, as in v. 28 (EVV v. 27). However, Ps. 68 is clearly making here a direct allusion to the tradition we now have in the Song of Deborah, and certainly does not indicate or support a cultic origin for this tradition.

17. The division of the Song adopted here differs from that proposed by Richter, *Richterbuch*, pp. 91f. The latter would put the beginning of the Song at v. 6 which, with vv. 7–8, sets the context for what follows. However, Richter's view is seriously weakened by the fact that he feels forced to propose (*ibid.*, p. 83) that v. 12 should come before v. 9, v. 9 being the beginning of the song which Deborah in v. 12 is called upon to sing. It is clear that v. 12, with its series of imperatives, does, as Richter says (*ibid.*, p. 95), begin something new. For the view adopted here, cf. Müller, *VT* 16, 1966. pp. 446ff. The latter, however, also argues (*VT* 16, 1966, pp. 453ff.) that the Song has been subjected to a double 'Yahwistic editing', the first including vv. 2f., and the second in vv. 9–11, 31a.

18. Richter. *Richterbuch*. p. 110, conjectures that the reception of the Song into the cult as a hymn of praise to Yahweh took place in Jerusalem; cf. also Müller, *VT* 16, 1966, pp. 458f.

19. So Richter, *Richterbuch*, pp. 95f.

20. Cf. Craigie, *JBL* 88, 1969, pp. 259f.; and also Nyström, *Beduinentum und Jahwismus*, pp. 53f., who notes that the bedouin in war made use of magical sayings, the author of which was as much a participant in the battle as the warrior. He finds parallels to this in the Old Testament story of Balaam and in this case of Deborah. One could perhaps also compare this with the part played by Moses in the story of the battle against Amalek, cf. Ex. 17.8–13.

21. Just as Jael was a non-Israelite but belonged to a clan (the Kenites) closely associated with the Israelites, and so was particularly worthy of a blessing for her action, so it would appear that Meroz must likewise have been a non-Israelite city but closely associated with Israel, probably in the form of a covenant, and so was especially worthy of being cursed for its non-participation in the battle. It would seem that it is the contrast with Jael which

dictated the curse to be pronounced on Meroz, rather than any treachery on the part of Meroz more to be condemned than the absence of the tribes mentioned in vv. 15–17 which are not cursed. The use of contrasts in the structure of the Song is emphasized by Gerleman, *VT* i, 1951, pp. 172ff.

22. Cf. also Nyström, *Beduinentum und Jahwismus*, pp. 45ff.

23. Cf. also Smend, *Yahweh War and Tribal Confederation*, p. 14, n. 3. The argument of Noth, *History of Israel*, p. 150, n. 3, that there has been a secondary extension of the number of tribes mentioned as having taken part in the battle, cannot, as noted already, be supported by reference to Judg. 4, nor is it at all likely in view of the way in which these tribes are referred to in the Song.

24. For references and other details on this and what follows, see my article in *VT* 19, 1969, pp. 353ff.

25. For this, cf. Alt, *Kleine Schriften* i, pp. 256ff.

26. Cf. above p. 76.

27. Cf. Alt, *Kleine Schriften* i, pp. 261f.

28. Alt, *ibid.*, p. 266. On Sisera as a Philistine or at least as one of the 'Sea Peoples' who first appeared in Palestine about 1200 BC, cf. also Noth, *History of Israel*, p. 150; Graham and May, *Culture and Conscience*, p. 150. However, cf. Aharoni, in *Near Eastern Archaeology in the Twentieth Century*, pp. 257, 264f.

29. Alt, *Kleine Schriften* i, p. 270.

30. Against Alt, cf. also Aharoni, in *Near Eastern Archaeology in the Twentieth Century*, pp. 254ff. Aharoni, however, proposes a date in the late thirteenth or early twelfth century for the victory over Sisera. His reasons are (*a*) 'Shamgar Ben-anath was a military leader of Canaanite origin who was led to smite the Philistines by the inspiration of Jael.' And the Philistines smitten by Shamgar were Egyptian mercenaries known from pottery discoveries to have been present at Beth-shan towards the end of the thirteenth century. (*b*) The situation reflected in the Song of Deborah, which refers to Machir, is earlier than that reflected in Judg. 1.27. which refers to Manasseh; yet the latter must come from a time before the destruction of Taanach which, from the evidence of archaeology, took place *c.* 1125 BC. Against this, however, it should be noted: (*a*) that Aharoni's argument that the only definite evidence we have of Philistines so far north in the early time is provided by the Beth-shan pottery remains of the thirteenth century, and that Shamgar must therefore be dated to that time, is not exactly watertight. In the first place, it is primarily an argument *e silentio*, and, secondly, Shamgar's area of activity cannot really be pinpointed. (*b*) The impression given by Judg. 3.31 is certainly not that Shamgar's opponents were Egyptian mercenaries. (*c*) If Aharoni is right in associating Shamgar and Jael in the way that he does, which is not really supported by the text, the historical reconstruction which results is, as Aharoni himself admits, that a successful coalition of Israelites and Canaanites against the Philistines broke up immediately after the defeat of the Philistines and the two former partners engaged each other in battle. This in itself is perhaps not unlikely, but it is unlikely that two such battles, one between the coalition and the Philistines and the other between the partners in the coalition, should be commemorated in the same Song. (*d*) It could easily be the case that Judg. 1.27 referred originally to Machir, but that after Machir became known only as a tribe living in east Jordan the tradition

was modified to refer to Manasseh the new inhabitant of the region. Finally, Aharoni's proposal means that the victory would have taken place when both Taanach and Megiddo were strong Canaanite fortresses (cf. *ibid.*, p. 260); it is much more likely, however, that a basic presupposition of the Israelite victory was a decline in power of these cities if not indeed the abandonment of them.

31. Cf. Noth, *History of Israel*, p. 165. Bright, *History*, p. 181, puts the battle 'sometime after 1050 BC'; cf. also Albright, in *The Old Testament and Modern Study*, p. 12, n. 3.

32. The argument of Albright, *BASOR* 68, 1937, p. 25; Aharoni, in *Near Eastern Archaeology in the Twentieth Century*, pp. 263ff., that Megiddo VI was an Israelite settlement, is contradicted by the biblical tradition in Judg. 1.27f. and, furthermore, is not demanded by the archaeological evidence which is brought forward; pieces similar to what has been taken as Israelite pottery were found already in Megiddo VII, cf. Alt, *Kleine Schriften* 1, pp. 264f. The presence of such pottery may simply attest outside influence or it may only represent the fashion of a particular age rather than be evidence of a change in occupation of the city. On the whole subject, cf. Weippert, *The Settlement of the Israelite Tribes in Palestine*, pp. 133ff.

33. It was probably also as a result of this defeat that Ephraimites were forced northwards to displace a large part of the tribe of Machir which eventually settled in Gilead; cf. above pp. 28f.

34. According to Alt, *Essays*, p. 167. Shunem would also have belonged to this system of city-states originally, but was destroyed in the time of Amenophis III by Labaya, and was not restored. This enabled the tribe of Issachar to settle in the area of Shunem and Jezreel, though still, evidently, at the cost of its political independence.

35. Cf. Aharoni, in *Near Eastern Archaeology in the Twentieth Century*, p. 260.

36. Cf. Alt, *Kleine Schriften* 1, pp. 257ff.

37. On Gilead as a tribal name here, cf. above p. 30.

38. Cf. above pp. 28ff.

39. Cf. Mowinckel, *Quellen in Josua 13–19*, p. 21; *idem*, in *Von Ugarit nach Qumran*, p. 137; cf. also Weiser, *ZAW* 71, 1959, p. 96, who is followed by Schunck, *Benjamin*, pp. 52f. See also Weippert, *VT* 23, 1973, pp. 76ff.

40. Cf. Mendenhall, *The Tenth Generation*, pp. 1ff., 28ff., 179ff.

41. Simeon seems very early to have been absorbed into Judah. In the descriptions of territory allotted to this tribe in Josh. 19.1ff., only a few cities within Judah are reckoned as Simeonite territory.

42. Cf. above pp. 2ff.; and Alt, *Essays*, pp. 173ff., 241ff. On the establishment of the worship of Yahweh in Judah, cf. Clements, *Abraham and David*, pp. 38ff., 42f. See also further below, pp. 106ff.

43. Zobel, *Stammesspruch und Geschichte*, p. 76, suggests that the reason for the silence of the Song of Deborah on Judah is to be found in Judah's arrogant claim to be considered as leader of the tribes, a claim which is reflected in Gen. 49.10–12 (these verses are dated by Zobel to the period immediately following the battle against Siseral). However, there is no other evidence of such an attitude on the part of Judah in this early period, and, since the date of these verses is far from undisputed, it would seem best to place them in a

period which would, according to the evidence we do possess, form a suitable historical context, i.e. probably the early monarchy period.

44. Cf. Meyer, *Die Israeliten und ihre Nachbarstämme*, pp. 75ff., 232f.; Alt, *Essays*, pp. 166f.; Smend, *Yahweh War and Tribal Confederation*, p. 17; Herrmann, *TLZ* 87, 1962, col. 569.

45. See now also de Vaux, in *Translating and Understanding the Old Testament*, pp. 108ff.

46. In Josh. 10.36f., Hebron is said to have been taken by Joshua; it has been suggested by Wright, *JNES* 5, 1946, pp. 105ff. (cf. also Gold, in *IDB* 2, p. 576), that after Hebron was taken by Joshua it had to be reconquered at a later stage by Caleb. However, this seems an unlikely solution, cf. further below, and Clements, *Abraham and David*, p. 42.

47. Joshua has been brought into this context by P; cf. Num. 14.24, and Noth, *Überlieferungsgeschichtliche Studien*, p. 203, n. 6. For what follows here, cf. Noth, *History of Pentateuchal Traditions*, pp. 130ff.

48. On the identification of the sites of these cities, cf. Mazar, *IsrEJ* 10, 1960, pp. 65ff.; Strange, *ST* 19, 1965, pp. 120ff.

49. For the use of the term 'Amorite', cf. Noth, *Die Ursprünge des alten Israel im Lichte neuer Quellen*, p. 27; and the detailed study by van Seters, *VT* 22, 1972, pp. 64ff.

50. According to Judg. 1.8, the men of Judah captured Jerusalem; but in view of v. 21 of the same chapter, and since Judg. 19.10ff. presents Jerusalem as a still Jebusite city, it is best to see Judg. 1.8 as a reflection of conditions during and after the time of David whose capture of the city is related in II Sam. 5.6ff. On Gezer, cf. Judg. 1.29; I Kings 9.16. For an explanation of Judg. 1.8, which does not involve treating the verse as anachronistic, cf. Gray, *Joshua, Judges and Ruth*, p. 247.

51. If Deut. 33.7 derives from the period of the judges (cf. Schunck, *Benjamin*, p. 72; Smend, in *Fourth World Congress of Jewish Studies*, pp. 61f.), it would harmonize well with the conditions outlined here. This verse would express the desire of Judah, now separated from the other tribes, to be brought into contact with them. The reference to the 'adversaries' would then probably mean the inhabitants of those city-states which cut Judah off from access to the north.

52. On Judah as an addition to the tradition of Judg. 19–21, cf. above pp. 8of.

53. The time of Dan's migration to the north (cf. Judg. 17–18) cannot be determined with certainty. However, it is probable that if this was a result of Philistine pressure it took place not long after the settlement of the Philistines in about 1200 BC. Judges 1.34, however, relates that it was the Amorites who would not allow Dan to occupy this area, which would mean that this Danite bridge between Judah and the north was of extremely short duration; cf. Noth, *History of Israel*, pp. 67f.; Rowley, *From Joseph to Joshua*, pp. 84f. On the question of where Dan in the Song of Deborah is presupposed as living see my article *VT* 19, 1969, p. 355, n. 1.

54. Cf. above p. 3.

55. Aijalon is named in Judg. 1.35 as one of the foreign city-states unconquered by Israel, which separated Judah from the north.

56. On this, cf. Hauer, *CBQ* 31, 1969, pp.153ff.
57. This is rightly emphasized by Noth, *System*, pp.62f.
58. Cf. Clements, *Abraham and David*, pp.25ff.
59. Josh.22 tells of the establishment of such a sanctuary, but the story is late, and it is uncertain, if it is in any way historically reliable in the matter at issue here. According to McKenzie, *The World of the Judges*, p.7, the chapter 'approaches midrash; it is a priestly narrative stating the law of the unity of the sanctuary'; but cf. Wildberger, *Jahwes Eigentumsvolk*, p.68, who thinks that the chapter may have a historical basis.
60. Cf. above p.30.
61. The researches of Alt and Noth, which have greatly illuminated Israel's early history in many respects, have, nevertheless, resulted in what seems to be an unjustifiable emphasis on the element of discontinuity between the period of the judges and the monarchic state, to the extent that the monarchy is sometimes seen as an alien institution imposed on the true people of Yahweh. If the representation given here is correct, the monarchy should rather be seen as a natural development from the process of the tribes' striving for political unity throughout the earlier period. For points of contact between the monarchy and the period of the judges, cf. Buccellati, *Cities and Nations of Ancient Syria*, pp.101, 210ff., 240ff.; and Langlamet, *RB* 77, 1970, pp.161ff.

Chapter IV

1. Cf. my article, in *Hermathena* 110, 1970, pp.42ff.
2. Cf. Noth, *The Laws in the Pentateuch*, pp.132ff.
3. A particular connection of Jerusalem with north Israelite cultic tradition has been argued for on the basis of the presence in Jerusalem of the ark, which had been a cultic symbol venerated by the northern tribes in the context of the Exodus and Sinai covenant traditions. However, an exclusive association of these sacral traditions with the ark is ruled out by the absence of the ark from the sanctuary at Shechem. Furthermore, any discussion of the significance of the ark must take account of the fact that it lay abandoned at Kiriath-jearim before being brought to Jerusalem by David, although it is possible that Philistine control of Kiriath-jearim may explain this; cf. Jacob, *La tradition historique en Israel*, pp.74f.; Eissfeldt, VTS 4, 1956. p.142; Fretheim, *JBL* 86, 1967. p.296. On the significance of the ark, cf. also Clements, *God and Temple*, pp.28ff.; von Rad, *The Problem of the Hexateuch*, p.103ff. According to Newman, *The People of the Covenant*, pp.61ff., 125f., 151, 161, the ark had been closely associated with the E covenant legend, but this connection was broken when the ark was captured by the Philistines.
4. On this, cf. particularly Alt, *Essays*, pp.217f., 233f., 247ff., 254ff.
5. Cf. especially Clements, *Abraham and David*, pp.42f.
6. Noth, *History of Pentateuchal Traditions*, pp.133f., thinks that Hormah was the starting point of the movement northwards of the Calebites. However, it seems to me that the Hormah tradition should be treated as an independent one parallel to the Hebron tradition. Just as Caleb's settlement of

Hebron has now become part of the settlement of all Israel, so that its conquest is a conquest of all Israel following an invasion from the east under Joshua, so the independent settlement of Hormah by a small group, probably Simeonites (cf. Judg. 1.17), has now come into a context in which it was conquered by all Israel in the course of its wanderings, cf. Num. 21.1–3. Undoubtedly, one should think of several independent movements into the southern part of the land, and not just that of Caleb; cf. also Alt, *Kleine Schriften* 3, pp. 427ff.

7. On Kadesh, cf. for example, Meyer, *Die Israeliten und ihre Nachbarstämme*, pp. 60, 63ff., 79ff.; Wellhausen, *Prolegomena to the History of Israel*, pp. 430ff.; Eissfeldt, in *CAH* II ch. xxvi (*a*), pp. 19ff. As far as the relationship of Kadesh and Sinai is concerned, it is undoubtedly true that the Sinaitic traditions are an intrusion into the Kadesh cycle of traditions, cf. von Rad, *The Problem of the Hexateuch*, p. 14. But since Sinai was not only the mountain of Yahweh's revelation, but was probably also the abode of Yahweh to which regular pilgrimages were made, cf. Clements, *God and Temple*, p. 19 (and, for the route of pilgrimages to Sinai in later time, cf. Noth, *PJB* 36, 1940, pp. 5ff.), and since Kadesh was a centre of wandering tribes which worshipped Yahweh, it is clear that there is some historical connection between Kadesh and Sinai even if this connection cannot be precisely defined.

8. It is unlikely that Caleb was the only group which came into this area as worshippers of Yahweh. However, the traditions about Caleb are clearer than those of other Judean clans. For these others, cf. de Vaux, in *Translating and Understanding the Old Testament*, pp. 108ff., where it is also argued that these southern groups had pre-settlement contact with those who came out of Egypt with Moses.

9. Cf. above.

10. The worship of Yahweh at Shechem cannot adequately be explained on the supposition of the spread of Yahwism to the north through the work of the Levites. It is Joshua who celebrates the covenant at Shechem, and, furthermore, there is no indication of the participation of the Levites in the Shechemite cult in the period of the judges, cf. Clements, *VT* 17, 1967, pp. 128ff.

11. This can be accepted in its broad outline as what must have taken place in order to provide an explanation for the appearance of Yahwism both at Shechem and at Kadesh. We do not wish to deal here with the questions raised by Noth's view of the original independence of the Pentateuchal themes, in this case the wilderness wandering theme and the settlement theme in particular.

12. In view that the invasion from the south was a 'century or two earlier' than the incursion from the east (so Eissfeldt, in *CAH* II ch. xxvi (*a*), pp. 23f.), or that the invasion from the south took place in the Amarna age (so Rowley, *From Joseph to Joshua*, pp. 76f.), cannot be given any convincing demonstration. Against Rowley's interpretation of Num. 13.22b, cf. Clements, *Abraham and David*, p. 41.

BIBLIOGRAPHY

Abba, R., 'Priests and Levites', *IDB* 3, 1962, pp. 877–889.

Ackroyd, P. R., 'The Composition of the Song of Deborah', *VT* 2, 1952, pp. 160–162.

Aharoni, Y., 'The Province List of Judah', *VT* 9, 1959, pp. 225–246.

'New Aspects of the Israelite Occupation in the North', *Near Eastern Archaeology in the Twentieth Century*, Essays in Honor of Nelson Glueck, ed. J. A. Sanders, 1970. pp. 254–267.

Albright, W. F., 'Further Light on the History of Israel from Lachish and Megiddo', *BASOR* 68, 1937, pp. 22–26.

Archaeology and the Religion of Israel, 1942.

From the Stone Age to Christianity, 1957.

'The Old Testament and the Archaeology of Palestine', *The Old Testament and Modern Study*, ed. H. H. Rowley, 1961, pp. 1–26.

Yahweh and the Gods of Canaan, 1968.

Alt, A., 'Eine galiläische Ortsliste in Jos. 19', *ZAW* 45, 1927, pp. 59–81.

'Die Wallfahrt von Sichem nach Bethel', *Kleine Schriften zur Geschichte des Volkes Israel* 1, 1953, pp. 79–88.

'Joshua', *Kleine Schriften* 1, pp. 176–192.

'Das System der Stammesgrenzen im Buche Josua', *Kleine Schriften* 1, pp. 193–202.

'Megiddo im Übergang vom kanaanäischen zum israelitischen Zeitalter', *Kleine Schriften* 1, pp. 256–273.

'Meros', *Kleine Schriften* 1, pp. 274–277.

'Judas Gaue unter Josia', *Kleine Schriften* 2, 1953, pp. 276–288.

'Galiläische Probleme', *Kleine Schriften* 2, pp. 363–435.

'Beiträge zur historischen Geographie und Topographie des Negeb', *Kleine Schriften* 3, 1959, pp. 382–459.

'The God of the Fathers', *Essays on Old Testament History and Religion*, 1966, pp. 1–77.

'The Origins of Israelite Law', *Essays*, pp. 79–132.

'The Settlement of the Israelites in Palestine', *Essays*, pp. 133–169.

'The Formation of the Israelite State in Palestine', *Essays*, pp. 171–237.

'The Monarchy in the Kingdoms of Israel and Judah', *Essays*, pp. 239–259.

Anderson, G. W., 'Israel: Amphictyony; 'AM; ḲĀHĀL; 'ĒDĀH', *Translating and Understanding the Old Testament*, Essays in Honor of H. G. May, ed. H. T. Frank and W. L. Reed, 1970, pp. 135–151.

Bächli, O., *Israel und die Völker*, ATANT 41, 1962.

Baltzer, K., *The Covenant Formulary*, 1971.

Barr, J., *Old and New in Interpretation*, 1966.

Bentzen, A., *Introduction to the Old Testament* 1, 1948.

Beyerlin, W., *Die Kulttraditionen Israels in der Verkündigung des Propheten Micha*, FRLANT 54, 1959.
  'Geschichte und heilsgeschichtliche Traditionsbildung im alten Testament (Richter vi–viii)', *VT* 13, 1963, pp. 1–25.
  'Gattung und Herkunft des Rahmens im Richterbuch', *Tradition und Situation*, A. Weiser Festschrift, ed. F. Würthwein and O. Kaiser, 1963, pp. 1–29.
  Origins and History of the Oldest Sinaitic Traditions, 1965.

Brekelmans, C., 'Die sogenannte deuteronomischen Elemente in Gen.-Num.', VTS 15, 1966, pp. 90–96.

Brekelmans, H. W., 'Exodus xviii and the Origins of Yahwism in Israel', *OTS* 10, 1954, pp. 215–224.

Bright, J., 'Introduction and Exegesis of Joshua', *IB* 2, 1953.
  Early Israel in Recent History Writing, SBT 19, 1956.
  A History of Israel ², 1972.

Buccellati, G., *Cities and Nations of Ancient Syria*, Studi Semitici 26, 1967.

Budde, K., *The Religion of Israel to the Exile*, 1899.

Buhl, M. L., and Holm-Nielsen, S., *Shiloh. The Danish Excavations at Tall Sailun, Palestine, in 1926, 1929, 1932, and 1963. The Pre-Hellenistic Remains*, Publications of the National Museum Archaeological-Historical Series I, XII, 1969.

Carmichael, C., 'A New View of the Origin of the Deuteronomic Credo', *VT* 19, 1969, pp. 273–289.

Cazelles, H., *Études sur le code de l'alliance*, 1946.

Childs, B. S., 'Deuteronomic Formulae of the Exodus Traditions', VTS 16, 1967, pp. 30–39.

Clements. R. E., *God and Temple*, 1965.
  Prophecy and Covenant, SBT 43, 1965.
  Abraham and David, SBT (Second Series) 5, 1967.
  Review of Gunneweg, *Leviten und Priester*, *VT* 17, 1967, pp. 128–130.

Cody, A., *A History of Old Testament Priesthood*, Analecta Biblica 35, 1969.

Coote, R. C., 'The Meaning of the Name Israel', *HTR* 65, 1972, pp. 137–142.

Coppens, J., 'La bénédiction de Jacob', VTS 4, 1956, pp. 97–115.

Craigie, P. C., 'The Song of Deborah and the Epic of Tukulti-Ninurta', *JBL* 88, 1969, pp. 253–265.

Cross, F. M., and Wright, G. E., 'The Boundary and Province Lists of the Kingdom of Judah', *JBL* 75, 1956, pp. 202–226.

Danell, G. A., *Studies in the Name Israel in the Old Testament*, 1946.

Davies, G. H., 'The Ark in the Psalms', *Promise and Fulfilment*, Essays presented to S. H. Hooke, ed. F. F. Bruce, 1963, pp. 51–61.

Driver, G. R., 'Sacred Numbers and Round Figures', *Promise and Fulfilment*, Essays presented to S. H. Hooke, ed. F.F. Bruce, 1963, pp. 62–90.

Driver, S. R., *Notes on the Hebrew Text of the Books of Samuel* ², 1960.

Eissfeldt, O., 'Der geschichtliche Hintergrund der Erzählung von Gibeas Schandtat (Richter 19–21)', *Festschrift Georg Beer*, ed. A. Weiser, 1935, pp. 19–40.

'Silo und Jerusalem', VTS 4, 1956, pp. 138–147.

The Old Testament. An Introduction, 1965.

'Palestine in the time of the Nineteenth Dynasty (a) the Exodus and Wanderings', *CAH* (revised edition) II ch. xxvi (a), 1965.

'The Hebrew Kingdom', *CAH* (revised edition) II ch. xxxiv, 1965.

Emerton, J. A., 'Some Difficult Words in Genesis 49', *Words and Meanings, Essays presented to D. Winton Thomas*, ed. P. R. Ackroyd and B. Lindars, 1968, pp. 81–93.

Fensham, F. C., 'The Judge and Ancient Israelite Jurisprudence', *OT Werk-SuidA* 1959, pp. 15ff.

Fohrer, G., '"Amphiktyonie" und "Bund"', *TLZ* 91, 1966, cols. 802–816, 893–904.

Introduction to the Old Testament, 1970.

Fretheim, T. E., 'Psalm 132. A Form-Critical Study', *JBL* 86, 1967, pp. 289–300.

Gelb, I. J., 'The Early History of the West Semitic Peoples', *JCS* 15, 1961, pp. 27–47.

Gerleman, G., 'The Song of Deborah in the Light of Stylistics', *VT* 1, 1951, pp. 168–180.

Glueck, N., 'Explorations in Eastern Palestine, III', *AASOR* xviii–xix, 1939.

Gold, V. R., 'Hebron', *IDB* 2, 1962, pp. 575–577.

Graham, W. C., and May, H. G., *Culture and Conscience*, 1936.

Gray, J., *Joshua, Judges and Ruth*, The Century Bible, 1967.

Grether, O., 'Die Bezeichnung Richter für die charismatischen Helden der vorstaatlichen Zeit', *ZAW* 57, 1939, pp. 110–121.

Grønbaek, J. H., 'Benjamin und Juda', *VT* 15, 1965, pp. 421–436.

Gunkel, H., *What Remains of the Old Testament*, 1928.

Gunneweg, A. H. J., *Leviten und Priester,* FRLANT 89, 1965.

Haag, H., 'Gideon-Jerubbaal-Abimelek', *ZAW* 79, 1967, pp. 305–314.

Haran, M., 'Zebaḥ Hayyamîm', *VT* 19, 1969, pp. 11–22.

Hauer, C. E., 'The Shape of Saulide Strategy', *CBQ* 31, 1969, pp. 153–167.

Herrmann, S., 'Das Werden Israels', *TLZ* 87, 1962, cols. 561–574.

'Neuere Arbeiten zur Geschichte Israels', *TLZ* 89, 1964, cols. 813–819.

Hertzberg, H. W., 'Die Entwicklung des Begriffes *mišpṭ* im Alten Testament', *ZAW* 40, 1922, pp. 256–287.

'Die kleinen Richter', *TLZ* 79, 1954, cols. 285–290.

Die Bücher Josua, Richter, Ruth, ATD 9, 1959.

Hoftijzer, J., 'Enige Opmerkingen rond het israëlitischen 12-Stammensysteem', *NedTTs* 14, 1959–60, pp. 241–263.

Holm-Nielsen, S., see Buhl, M. L.

Holmes, S., *Joshua, The Hebrew and Greek Texts*, 1914.

Horst, F., 'Recht und Religion im Bereich des Alten Testament', *Gottes Recht*, Theologische Bücherei 12, 1961, pp. 260–291.

'Bundesbuch', *RGG*[3] 1, cols. 1523–1525.

Horwitz, W. J., 'Were there Twelve Horite Tribes?', *CBQ* 35, 1973, pp. 69–71.

Hvidberg, F. F., *Weeping and Laughter in the Old Testament*, 1962.

Hyatt, J. P., 'Were there an Ancient Historical Credo in Israel and an Independent Sinai Tradition?', *Translating and Understanding the Old Testament*, Essays in Honor of H. G. May, ed. H. T. Frank and W. L. Reed, 1970, pp. 152–170.

Irwin, W. H., 'Le sanctuaire central israélite avant l'établissement de la monarchie', *RB* 72, 1965, pp. 161–184.

Jacob, E., *La tradition historique en Israel*, 1946.

Johnson, A. R., 'Hebrew Conceptions of Kingship', *Myth, Ritual and Kingship*, ed. S. H. Hooke, 1958, pp. 204–235.
*Sacral Kingship in Ancient Israel*², 1967.

Kaiser, O., 'Stammesgeschichtliche Hintergründe der Josephsgeschichte', *VT* 10, 1960, pp. 1–15.

Kassis, H. E., 'Gath and the Structure of the Philistine Society', *JBL* 84, 1965, pp. 259–271.

Kaufmann, Y., *The Religion of Israel from its Beginnings to the Babylonian Exile*, 1961.

Keller, C. A., 'Über einige alttestamentliche Heiligtumslegenden, II', *ZAW* 68, 1956, pp. 85–97.

Kjaer, H., 'The Danish Excavation of Shiloh', *PEQ* 59, 1927, pp. 202–213.

Knierim, R., 'Exodus 18 und die Neuordnung der mosaischen Gerichtsbarkeit', *ZAW* 73, 1961, pp. 146–171.

Koch, K., *The Growth of the Biblical Tradition*, 1969.

Köhler, L., *Hebrew Man*, 1956.

Köhler, L., and Baumgartner, W., *Lexicon in Veteris Testamenti Libros*, 1953; Supplementum, 1958.

Kraus, H. J., 'Gilgal. Ein Beitrag zur Kultusgeschichte Israels', *VT* 1, 1951, pp. 181–199.
Die prophetische Verkündigung des Rechts in Israel, Theologische Studien 51, 1957.
Worship in Israel, 1966.

Langlamet, F., 'Les récits de l'institution de la royauté (I Sam. vii–xii)', *RB* 77, 1970, pp. 161–200.

Lehming, S., 'Zur Erzählung von der Geburt der Jakobsöhne', *VT* 13, 1963, pp. 74–81.

L'Hour, J., 'L'alliance de Sichem', *RB* 69, 1962, pp. 5–36, 161–184, 350–368.

Lindars, B., 'Gideon and the Kingship', *JTS* 16, 1965, pp. 315–326.

Lindblom, J., 'The Political Background of the Shiloh Oracle', VTS 1, 1953, pp. 78–87.

Lohfink, N., *Das Hauptgebot. Eine Untersuchung literarischer Einleitungsfragen zu Dtn 5–11*, Analecta Biblica 20, 1963.

McCarthy, D. J., *Treaty and Covenant*, Analecta Biblica 21, 1963.
Old Testament Covenant, 1972.

McKenzie, D. A., 'The Judge of Israel', *VT* 17, 1967, pp. 118–121.

McKenzie, J. L., *The World of the Judges*, 1967.

Maier, J., *Das altisraelitische Ladeheiligtum*, BZAW 93, 1965.

Margulis, B., 'An Exegesis of Judg. v 8a', *VT* 15, 1965, pp. 66–72.

May, H. G., see Graham, W. C.

Mayes, A. D. H., 'The Historical Context of the Battle against Sisera', *VT* 19, 1969, pp. 353–360.

'The Covenant on Sinai and the Covenant with David', *Hermathena* 110, 1970, pp. 37–51.

Mazar, B., 'The Cities of the Territory of Dan', *IsrEJ* 10, 1960, pp. 65–77.

Mendenhall, G. E., 'Ancient Oriental and Biblical Law', *BA* 17, 1954, pp. 26–46.

'The Census Lists of Num. 1 and 26', *JBL* 77, 1958, pp. 52–66.

'The Relation of the Individual to Political Society in Ancient Israel', *Biblical Studies in Memory of H. C. Alleman*, ed. J. M. Myers, O. Reimheer and H. N. Bream, 1960, pp. 89–108.

'The Hebrew Conquest of Palestine', *BA* 25, 1962, pp. 66–87.

The Tenth Generation. The Origins of the Biblical Tradition, 1973.

Meyer, E., *Die Israeliten und ihre Nachbarstämme*, 1967.

Möhlenbrink, K., 'Die Landnahmesagen des Buches Josua', *ZAW* 56, 1938, pp. 238–268.

Moore, G. E., *Judges*, ICC, 1895.

Mowinckel, S., *Le décalogue*, 1927.

Zur Frage nach dokumentarischen Quellen in Josua 13–19, ANVAO 2 Hist.-Filos, Klasse, 1946.

'"Rahelstämme" und "Leastämme"', *Von Ugarit nach Qumran*[2], O. Eissfeldt Festschrift, ed. J. Hempel and L. Rost, BZAW 77, 1961, pp. 129–150.

'Israelite Historiography', *ASTI* 2, 1963, pp. 4–26.

Tetrateuch-Pentateuch-Hexateuch. Die Berichte über die Landnahme bei den drei altisraelitischen Geschichtswerken, BZAW 90, 1964.

Muilenburg, J., 'Mizpah of Benjamin', *ST* 8, 1955, pp. 25–42.

'The Form and Structure of the Covenantal Formulations', *VT* 9, 1959, pp. 347–365.

'The "Office" of the Prophet in Ancient Israel', *The Bible in Modern Scholarship*, ed. J. P. Hyatt, 1966, pp. 74–97.

Müller, H. P., 'Der Aufbau des Deboraliedes', *VT* 16, 1966, pp. 446–459.

Newman, M., *The People of the Covenant*, 1965.

Nicholson, E. W., *Deuteronomy and Tradition*, 1967.

Nielsen, E., *Shechem. A Traditio-Historical Investigation*, 1955.

'The Burial of the Foreign Gods', *ST* 8, 1955, pp. 103–122.

The Ten Commandments in New Perspective, SBT (Second Series) 7, 1968.

Noth, M., *Die israelitischen Personennamen im Rahmen der gemeinsemitischen Namengebung*, BWANT III.10, 1928.

Das System der zwölf Stämme Israels, BWANT IV.1, 1930.

'Studien zu den historisch-geographischen Dokumenten des Josuabuches', *ZDPV* 58, 1935, pp. 185–255.

'Der Wallfahrtsweg zum Sinai (4 Mose 33)', *PJB* 36, 1940, pp. 5–28.

'Das Amt des Richters Israels', *Bertholet Festschrift*, ed. W. Baumgartner, O. Eissfeldt, K. Elliger and L. Rost, 1950, pp. 404–417.

'Überlieferungsgeschichtliches zur zweiten Hälfte des Josuabuches', *Alttestamentliche Studien Friedrich Nötscher zum 60.Geburtstag gewidmet*, BBB 1, 1950, pp. 152–167.

*Das Buch Josua*², HAT, 1953.

*Überlieferungsgeschichtliche Studien*², 1957.

'Gilead und Gad', *ZDPV* 75, 1959, pp. 14–73.

*The History of Israel*², 1960.

Die Ursprünge des alten Israel im Lichte neuer Quellen, Arbeitsgemeinschaft für Forschung des Landes Nordrhein-Westfalen, Heft 94, 1961.

'The Background of Judges 17–18', *Israel's Prophetic Heritage*, ed. B. W. Anderson and W. Harrelson, 1962, pp. 68–85.

'The Laws in the Pentateuch: their Assumptions and Meaning', *The Laws in the Pentateuch and Other Essays*, 1966, pp. 1–107.

'Jerusalem and the Israelite Tradition', *The Laws in the Pentateuch and Other Essays*, pp. 132–144.

'Office and Vocation in the Old Testament', *The Laws in the Pentateuch and Other Essays*, pp. 229–249.

The Old Testament World, 1966.

A History of Pentateuchal Traditions, 1972.

Nyström, S., *Beduinentum und Jahwismus*, 1946.

Orlinsky, H. M., 'The Tribal System of Israel and Related Groups in the Period of the Judges', *Studies and Essays in Honor of A. A. Neuman*, ed. M. Ben-Horin, B. D. Weinryb and S. Zeitlin, 1962, pp. 375–387.

Ottoson, M., *Gilead*, Coniectanea Biblica, Old Testament Series 3, 1969.

Pearce, R. A., 'Shiloh and Jer. VII 12, 14 & 15', *VT* 23, 1973, pp. 105–108.

Pedersen, J., *Israel* III–IV, 1940.

Perlitt, L., *Bundestheologie im Alten Testament*, WMANT 36, 1969.

Phillips, A., *Ancient Israel's Criminal Law*, 1970.

van der Ploeg, J., 'Les chefs du peuple d'Israel et leurs titres', *RB* 57, 1950, pp. 40–61.

Porteous, N. W., 'Actualization and the Prophetic Criticism of the Cult', *Tradition und Situation*, A. Weiser Festschrift, ed. E. Wurthwein and O. Kaiser, 1963, pp. 93–105.

Porter, J. R., *Moses and Monarchy*, 1963.

'The Background of Joshua III–V', *SEÅ* 36, 1971, pp. 5–23.

Pritchard, J. B. (ed.), *Ancient Near Eastern Texts*, 1950.

von Rad, G., *Der heilige Krieg im alten Israel*, ATANT 20, 1951.

Studies in Deuteronomy, SBT 9, 1953.

Old Testament Theology 1, 1962, 2, 1965.

'The Form-Critical Problem of the Hexateuch', *The Problem of the Hexateuch and Other Essays*, 1966, pp. 1–78.

'The Promised Land and Yahweh's Land in the Hexateuch', *The Problem of the Hexateuch and Other Essays*, pp. 79–93.

'The Tent and the Ark', *The Problem of the Hexateuch and Other Essays*, pp. 103–124.

Rahtjen, B. D., 'Philistine and Hebrew Amphictyonies', *JNES* 24, 1965, pp. 100–104.

Rendtorff, R., 'Reflections on the Early History of Prophecy in Israel', *History and Hermeneutic*, 1967, pp. 14–34.

Graf Reventlow, H., 'Kultisches Recht im alten Testament', *ZTK* 60, 1963, pp. 267–304.

Richter, W., 'Zu den "Richtern Israels" ', *ZAW* 77, 1965, pp. 40–72.

Traditionsgeschichtliche Untersuchungen zum Richterbuch², BBB 18, 1966.

Rowley, H. H., *From Joseph to Joshua* (Schweich Lectures 1948), 1950.

Rudolph, W., *Der 'Elohist' von Exodus bis Josua*, BZAW 68, 1938.

Schmidt, W., *Königtum Gottes in Ugarit und Israel*, BZAW 80, 1961.

Schmitt, G., *Der Landtag von Sichem*, 1964.

Schmökel, H., 'Jahwe und die Keniter', *JBL* 52, 1933, pp. 212–229.

Schunck, K. D., *Benjamin. Untersuchungen zur Entstehung und Geschichte eines israelitischen Stammes*, BZAW 86, 1963.

'Die Richter Israels und ihr Amt', VTS 15, 1966, pp. 252–262.

Seebass, H., *Der Erzvater Israel*, BZAW 98, 1966.

van Selms, A., 'The title "Judge" ', *OTWerkSuidA*, 1959, pp. 41ff.

'Judge Shamgar', *VT* 14, 1964, pp. 294–309.

van Seters, J., 'The terms "Amorite" and "Hittite" ', *VT* 22, 1972, pp. 64–81.

Smend, R., 'Gehörte Juda zum vorstaatlichen Israel?', *Fourth World Congress of Jewish Studies* 1, 1967, pp. 57–62.

Yahweh War and Tribal Confederation. Reflections upon Israel's Earliest History, 1970.

'Zur Frage der altisraelitischen Amphiktyonie', *EvT* 31, 1971, pp. 623–630.

Soggin, J. A., 'Zwei umstrittene Stellen aus dem Überlieferungskreis um Schechem', *ZAW* 73, 1961, pp. 78–87.

Das Königtum in Israel, BZAW 104, 1967.

Joshua, Old Testament Library, 1972.

Speiser, E. A., 'Background and Function of the Biblical Nāśī', *CBQ* 25, 1963, pp. 111–117.

Steuernagel, C., 'Jahwe und die Vätergötter', *Festschrift Georg Beer*, ed. A. Weiser, 1935, pp. 62–71.

Stoebe, H. J., 'Jakobsegen', *RGG³* 3, cols. 524–525.

Stolz, F., *Jahwes und Israels Kriege*, ATANT 60, 1972.

Strange, J., 'The Inheritance of Dan', *ST* 19, 1965, pp. 120–139.

Täubler, E., *Biblische Studien. Die Epoche der Richter*, herausg. von H. J. Zobel, 1958.

Thomson, H. C., 'Shopheṭ and Mishpaṭ in the Book of Judges', *TGUOS* 19, 1961–62, pp. 74–85.

de Vaux, R., *Ancient Israel. Its Life and Institutions*, 1961.

'The Settlement of the Israelites in Southern Palestine and the Origins of the Tribe of Judah', *Translating and Understanding the Old Testament*, Essays in Honor of H. G. May, ed. H. T. Frank and W. L. Reed, 1970, pp. 108–134.

'La thèse de l' "amphictyonie israélite" ', *HTR* 64, 1971, pp. 415–436.

Histoire ancienne d'Israel, 1971.

Volz, P., *Mose und sein Werk²*, 1932.

Vriezen, T. C., *The Religion of Ancient Israel*, 1967.

Weippert, H., 'Das geographische System der Stämme Israels', *VT* 23, 1973, pp. 76–89.

Weippert, M., *The Settlement of the Israelite Tribes in Palestine*, SBT (Second Series) 21, 1971.

' "Heiliger Krieg" in Israel und Assyrien', *ZAW* 84, 1972, pp. 460–493.

Weiser, A., 'Das Deboralied', *ZAW* 71, 1959, pp. 67–97.

    Introduction to the Old Testament, 1961.

    Samuel. Seine geschichtliche Aufgabe und religiöse Bedeutung, FRLANT 81, 1962.

    The Psalms, Old Testament Library, 1966.

Weiss, M., 'The Origin of the "Day of the Lord" – Reconsidered', *HUCA* 37, 1966, pp. 29–60.

Wellhausen, J., *Prolegomena to the History of Israel,* 1885.

Wildberger, H., *Jahwes Eigentumsvolk,* ATANT 37, 1960.

Willis, J. T., 'Micah iv 14–v 5 – a Unit', *VT* 18, 1968, pp. 529–547.

    'Cultic Elements in the Story of Samuel's Birth and Dedication', *ST* 26, 1972, pp. 33–61.

Wright, G. E., 'The Literary and Historical Problems of Joshua 10 and Judges 1', *JNES* 5, 1946, pp. 105–114.

    see Cross, F. M.

    Shechem. The Biography of a Biblical City, 1965.

Zobel, H. J., *Stammesspruch und Geschichte,* BZAW 95, 1965.

INDEX OF AUTHORS

References are to page and note numbers in each case
e.g. 115.29 = page 115, note 29

INDEX OF BIBLICAL REFERENCES